Electricity and Electronics Technology

INFORMATION PROCESSING SKILLS:

READING

Electricity and Electronics Technology

INFORMATION PROCESSING SKILLS:

READING

Thomas G. Sticht
Barbara A. McDonald

GOALS
Glencoe Occupational Adult Learning Series

GLENCOE

Macmillan/McGraw-Hill

New York, New York   Columbus, Ohio   Mission Hills, California   Peoria, Illinois

This program was prepared with the assistance of
Chestnut Hill Enterprises, Inc.

**Electricity and Electronics Technology Information
Processing Skills: Reading**

Send all inquiries to:

GLENCOE DIVISION
Macmillan/McGraw-Hill
936 Eastwind Drive
Westerville, OH 43081

ISBN: 0-07-061526-8

1 2 3 4 5 6 7 8 9 0   POH   99 98 97 96 95 94 93 92

Table of Contents

Preface

People used to think that when they got out of school, they could stop learning. Today, that is no longer true!

People who want careers in well-paying jobs have to use their knowledge and skills to learn every day. They have to keep up with rapid changes in technology. They must meet new demands for goods and services from customers. They have to compete for good jobs with workers from around the world.

The books in this program will help you learn how to learn. The *Electricity and Electronics Technology Knowledge Base* will give you the background you need to learn about electricity and electronics. The *Reading and Mathematics Information: Processing Skills* books will teach you how to use your skills to learn new information.

When you complete these three books, you will be ready for more training in the field of electricity and electronics. Then when you start your career, you will be able to learn new knowledge and skills. This way, you will always be able to keep up with changes in jobs. You will also be ready to move ahead to jobs of greater responsibility.

We wish you the very best of success in your chosen career field!

INTRODUCTION

The ability to read is one of the most important, most useful skills you can have. Reading is becoming more important every day. The reason is simple: No matter what kind of work you do, you *must* be able to read to do your job well.

❏ READING ON THE JOB

Today's world is an information world. The entire world is connected by a communications network using the technology of electricity and electronics. You may work at a telephone company, a computer repair shop, a manufacturer, or a power plant. What you read on the job depends on the kind of work you do. You may read many letters and memos. Perhaps you will read charts and graphs. You may need to read reports and manuals. Chances are, you will need to read many different kinds of materials. Whatever you do, you will need good reading skills.

SELF-CHECK 1-1

Directions: If you now work, take a separate sheet of paper and list the kinds of materials that you read on your job.

❏ THE IMPORTANCE OF GOOD READING SKILLS

Good reading skills will make your work easier. When you can apply good reading skills, you will be able to find answers to on-the-job questions. You will be able to solve on-the-job problems.

For example, when you learn to use parts of books, such as the table of contents, you will be able to find information in books very quickly. You will save time, but more important, you will be sure to find the right answers.

SELF-CHECK 1-2

Directions: In the space below, write three ways that good reading skills can help you in your job.

1. _____

2. _____

3. _____

SELF-CHECK 1-3

Directions: *In addition to the table of contents, can you name other parts of a book that might help you find something? Write your answers in the space below.*

_____

_____

This book and the *Electricity and Electronics Technology Knowledge Base* will help make your reading both easier and more effective by helping you to understand your reading goals. Let's see what this means.

❏ UNDERSTANDING YOUR GOALS

At times, you will read to *learn* something. Your goal will be to understand as many details of what you are reading as you can in order to master the information. At other times, you will read simply to *do* something—for example, to find an answer to a question. As you will see, reading to learn and reading to do are two very different goals, but both require reading skill.

READING TO LEARN

Assume that you must read a manual that describes how to use a new piece of equipment. The equipment can be dangerous if not used properly.

Of course, you want to learn as much about this equipment (especially its safety features) as you can. You want to *recall* the information you learn. That means that you want to be able to *use* the information in the future. You want to be able to apply what you read when you operate the equipment.

The information is important. Your purpose, your goal in reading, is to *master* the information. You want to keep the information in your permanent memory. Your goal is *reading to learn.*

READING TO DO

But you do not always read to master information. Sometimes, you will read simply to find an answer to a question or a problem. Once you find that answer, it really may not be important to *keep* the information in your memory at all.

For example, suppose you need to find the manufacturer's serial number for that same piece of equipment. You need to (1) find the number, (2) write it accurately on a form, and (3) give the filled-out form to your supervisor. Do you need to *memorize* the number? No. Do you need to *understand* it? No.

You simply need to *find* the number. It's somewhere in the 300-page manual that comes with the equipment. But you don't want to read every page of the manual just to find the number.

Of course, you *can* find the number quickly and easily. How? By using "finding tools" such as the table of contents in the manual. Your goal here is *reading to do*.

SELF-CHECK 1-4

Directions: *You have been asked to do the following tasks. In the space provided, put a check mark to indicate whether they are reading-to-learn or reading-to-do activities.*

Task	Reading to Learn	Reading to Do
1. Read a shipping chart to find the cost of mailing a three-pound package.	___	___
2. Read the instruction manual to learn how to use a multimeter.	___	___
3. Read a chapter in a textbook for a homework assignment.	___	___
4. Read a parts manual to find the number and cost of a part.	___	___
5. Read a telephone book to find a friend's number.	___	___
6. Read a manual to learn how to use a VCR.	___	___
7. Read a book about the Vietnam War.	___	___
8. Read the newspaper to find the score of last night's basketball game.	___	___
9. Read the newspaper to find out about an earthquake in California.	___	___
10. Read your *Electricity and Electronics Technology Knowledge Base.*	___	___

As you use this book together with your *Electricity and Electronics Technology Knowledge Base,* you will learn more about reading-to-learn and reading-to-do skills. First, let's look at the system your mind uses to process information. As you will see later, this will help you to use reading-to-learn and reading-to-do skills.

❏ INFORMATION PROCESSING

How do we learn? How does new information enter the memory? How does our brain remember? How does our mind store information and then find it again? In other words, how does the brain *process* information?

Understanding how we learn and how our brains process information will help you to improve your reading skills. To understand this process, let's begin by taking a look at the brain and its "inventory."

YOUR KNOWLEDGE BASE

Think of the information that is stored in your brain as your knowledge base. Your brain stores all kinds of information, including:

❏ Dates
❏ Statistics
❏ Pictures (of people's faces, of places, and of things, for example)
❏ Names
❏ Addresses
❏ Phone numbers

In other words, the total inventory in your brain, your total memory and knowledge, make up your knowledge base.

SELF-CHECK 1-5

Directions: *Write one example for each of the following items:*

1. *Dates* Write your date of birth. _____

2. *Statistics* Write your height and weight._____

3. *Pictures* Draw the flag of any country, and write the country's name to the right of it.

_____

4. *Names* Write the names of two of your friends. _____

_____

5. *Addresses* Write your address. _____

What, then, is "learning"? Learning is adding new information to your knowledge base—that is, adding to what you already know.

Stop for a moment to consider what is in *your* knowledge base. Think about one topic—bicycles. Take about five minutes to try to jot down everything you know about bicycles. Use the list that follows as a starting point. This is not a test—just a way of helping you to see how much information your brain has stored away about bicycles.

❏ All the experiences you have had riding, borrowing, racing, or repairing bicycles.

❏ All you know about bicycle gears—how they work, the names of the various types of bicycles, and what kind of terrain they cover.

❏ The names of different bicycle manufacturers, the popular types of bicycle clothing, and so on.

❏ Statistics about bicycles—safety, costs, exercise value, use of helmets, and so on.

❏ The kinds of bicycles your family, friends, and coworkers own and ride.

SELF-CHECK 1-6

Directions: *Jot down on a separate sheet of paper what you know about three of the following everyday topics. Spend about two minutes on each topic.*

1. Movies
2. Business
3. Finance
4. Sports
5. School
6. Advertising

Now choose *one* of the topics, and write what you know about it. Write three or four sentences in the space provided.

_____

_____

_____

_____

Don't be concerned about how much information you have stored away on these topics. Instead, think about how this information entered your brain and became part of your knowledge base. We are concerned with the *process* of learning.

IIOW YOUR BRAIN PROCESSES INFORMATION

Learning means adding new information to your knowledge base, adding to what you already know. The brain adds new information to your knowledge base in two different ways: by experience and by practice. Let's take a look at each.

EXPERIENCE. Whenever you see, taste, touch, hear, and talk, you remember some or all of that experience and store it in your knowledge base. For example, when you thought of bicycles earlier, you might have remembered:

1. Seeing a very fancy or unusual bicycle—or a picture of one.
2. Racing on your bicycle against your friends.
3. The feel of the wind on your face when riding your bicycle on a cold day.
4. Hearing a new horn on your brand-new mountain bike.
5. Talking with a friend about a biking trip or your bicycle.

SELF-CHECK 1-7

Directions: *Write a specific example, stored in your knowledge base, for each of the five experiences described above.*

1. _____

2. _____

3. _____

4. _____

5. _____

Each of these experiences is stored in your knowledge base. Your brain will also store other experiences, such as:

1. Seeing the exact words on a page.
2. Tasting a certain food.
3. Touching a soft fabric.
4. Hearing a favorite song or hearing a joke.
5. Talking to a friend or coworker about a certain topic.

No matter how the information gets there, your brain, or knowledge base, stores some information for a short time and some information for a long time. And once it is in your memory, you can use the information to help you learn more. You add to what is already stored in your brain.

Think of what might happen if you tried to drive a motorcycle for the first time. Would your earlier experience on a bicycle be helpful? Most likely it would be. If you were about to use a word processor for the first time, would your past experience on a typewriter be helpful? Sure it would be. In both instances, the "old" experience stored in your knowledge base would help you learn something new.

When you read, you can also use past experiences to help you understand what you are reading. If you are reading about a computer keyboard, you can use your experience with a typewriter keyboard to help you understand basic ideas.

PRACTICE. The more you use a piece of equipment that requires skill, the more you improve your skill. In other words, you learn through practice. For example, hammering nails becomes easier when you've repeated the process a few times. When you travel the same route day in, day out, for several months, the repetition helps you to learn that route.

As you will see, practice also helps you improve your reading skill. New, unknown words become familiar through practice, just as that travel route became familiar through practice.

SELF-CHECK 1-8

Directions: *Name five activities in which you improved your skill through practice.*

1. Activity: _____
2. Activity: _____
3. Activity: _____
4. Activity: _____
5. Activity: _____

P A R T

2

Reading to Do

LOCATING INFORMATION IN BOOKS

Books offer tools that help readers find information. The *Electricity and Electronics Technology Knowledge Base* has many of these tools. Working with this book and the *Knowledge Base*, you will learn about the following "finding tools":

❑ Table of Contents
❑ List of Figures
❑ Glossary
❑ Index

Each of these tools is described below.

❑ THE TABLE OF CONTENTS

The table of contents lists the major topics covered in a book. A portion of the contents from your *Electricity and Electronics Technology Knowledge Base* is shown in Figure 2-1.

Figure 2-1

The table of contents is always in the front of a book. It is usually in the first few pages. Find the *Electricity and Electronics Technology Knowledge Base* Table of Contents. What kind of information does it provide?

As you can see, it offers very useful information. The first part tells you where in the *Electricity and Electronics Technology Knowledge Base* you can find the Preface and the List of Figures.

Notice that the page numbers to the right of *Preface* and *List of Figures* are lowercase roman numerals. That is because they are in a part of the book called the *front matter*. The front matter is numbered separately from the main part of the book. The *Knowledge Base* Table of Contents is also part of the front matter. It is found on pages iii to v.

On the left side, the contents page shows both the title and the number of each chapter in the *Knowledge Base*. For example:

Chapter 1 Electricity and Electronics

Below each chapter title, you'll see a list of the subjects discussed in that chapter. For example:

Chapter 3 Repairing Electrical Items

(Topic 1) Electricity

(Topic 2) Electrical Repair

Just as the chapter titles tell you what's in the book, these subject listings tell you what's in each chapter.

Some subjects are divided into subtopics. Subtopics can also have their own subtopics. For example, look up Chapter 1 in the Table of Contents for the *Knowledge Base*. Chapter 1 is divided into three main topics:

(Topic 1) Working in Electricity and Electronics

(Topic 2) Jobs in Electricity and Electronics

(Topic 3) Technical Training

The first one of these main topics has subtopics. The section "Working in Electricity and Electronics" has two subsections:

(Topic 1) Working in Electricity and Electronics

(Subtopic 1) What is Electricity?

(Subtopic 2) What is Electronics?

Look at page 4 of the *Knowledge Base*. Notice that the main topic, "Working in Electricity and Electronics" appears larger than the subtopics, "What is Electricity?" and "What is Electronics?"

Look in the Table of Contents for the section in Chapter 6 called "Getting the Parts Together." It has four subtopics:

(Subtopic 1) Job Numbers

(Subtopic 2) Assembling the Parts

(Subtopic 3) Basic Wiring

(Subtopic 4) Inserting Printed Circuit Boards

The subtopic "Basic Wiring" has its own subtopics.

(Subtopic 1) Electrical Wire

(Subtopic 2) Connecting Wire

(Subtopic 3) Electronic Wire

Look at page 68 of the *Knowledge Base*. "Basic Wiring" is underlined. The subtopics to "Basic Wiring," on pages 69, 72 and 74, which can be referred to as "sub-subtopics," are not underlined. They also appear in smaller type than "Basic Wiring."

The page numbers in the Table of Contents (shown to the right of each chapter title and each section) tell you the first page of that chapter or section so that you can find it quickly.

Chapter 3 Repairing Electrical Items *21*

Now spend a few minutes looking over the Table of Contents in your *Electricity and Electronics Technology Knowledge Base*. Then do the following Self-Check.

SELF-CHECK 2-1

Directions: *Use the Table of Contents in the* Knowledge Base *to answer the following questions.*

1. How many chapters are there in the *Knowledge Base*? _____

2. What is the title of Chapter 6?

   _____

3. How many main topics are discussed in Chapter 6? _____

4. Name *all* the topics and subtopics in Chapter 6.

   _____

   _____

   _____

   _____

   _____

   _____

   _____

5. On which page does Chapter 2 begin? _____

6. In which chapter will you find information on:

Testers? _____

Making Purchases? _____

7. In a sentence or two, write about how a table of contents can help you locate information. _____

_____

_____

❏ THE LIST OF FIGURES

If a book has many tables, charts, and drawings, it may include a list of figures (illustrations) in the front. Find the page number for the List of Figures in the Table of Contents of your *Electricity and Electronics Technology Knowledge Base*. Turn to that page. Part of the List of Figures is shown in Figure 2-2 below.

Figure 2-2

The List of Figures gives the titles and page numbers of all the figures in the *Knowledge Base*. Like a chapter, each figure has a number and title. If you wanted to see a picture of capacitors, for example, you could use the List of Figures to find out what page it is on—instead of searching the whole book.

Every figure listed has two numbers that identify it. The first number tells you what chapter the figure is in; the second number tells you its order in the chapter. Each figure also has a title that describes its content. For example, in the list of figures, you find this:

Figure 3-6   *Making an electronic connection by soldering.*

That means that the picture that shows making a connection by soldering is the sixth illustration in Chapter 3.

SELF-CHECK 2-2

Directions: *Use the List of Figures in the* Knowledge Base *to answer the following questions.*

1. How many figures are there in Chapter 6? _____

2. Give the number of the figure that shows a computer monitor.

   _____

3. On what page will you find Figure 5-2? _____

4. Which chapter or chapters has the most figures? _____

5. Which chapter has an illustration of a testing checklist?_____

6. On what page is the last figure in the *Knowledge Base*? _____

7. In a sentence or two, write about how a list of figures can help you save time while you read._____

   _____

   _____

As you have just learned, the *Knowledge Base* contains many figures. It is often easier to find information in a figure than it is to find information in a paragraph or more of text. Look at Figure 3-3 on page 25 of the *Knowledge Base*.

The title appears beneath the illustration and tells you its subject. This figure is a photo of static electricity created in the hair. By looking at the figure and its title—also called a caption—you learn that a static electricity generator makes the hair stand straight up.

SELF-CHECK 2-3

Directions: *Use the figures indicated to answer the following questions.*

1. Figure 2-1 on page 14 of the *Knowledge Base*

   a. What is the marital status for the first two employees listed?

   _____

   b. What are the items that need to be filled in to complete the payroll register? _____

   _____

2. Figure 7-12 on page 89 of the *Knowledge Base*

    a. What is the product being tested? _____

    b. How many testing items must be checked? _____

    c. Who has to sign the checklist? _____

❑ THE GLOSSARY

A glossary is an alphabetized list of important terms in a book, accompanied by their definitions. Turn to the Table of Contents in the *Knowledge Base,* and find the page on which the Glossary begins. Then skim a few pages of the Glossary to get an idea of what it contains.

You use a glossary the same way you do a dictionary. If you don't understand a term, you can look it up. Remember, the Glossary contains only words or terms related to the *Electricity and Electronics Technology Knowledge Base.* Any words that appear in boldface, or heavy type, in the *Knowledge Base* are defined in the Glossary.

SELF-CHECK 2-4

Directions: *Read the following passage. Use the Glossary in the* Knowledge Base *to answer the questions that follow. (Circle the letter of each right answer.)*

Electricity is the field of technology that studies the movement of electrons. Electronics is the field of technology that deals with electrons moving along conductors. Conductors are materials or substances that make an easy path for the flow of electricity.

---

1. The term **electron** means:

    a. a machine that uses electricity

    b. a unit of measurement

    c. a particle inside an atom

2. The term **conductor** means:

    a. a battery cell

    b. a substance or material that allows electrical current to flow through it easily

    c. a type of electric current

3. The term **path** means:

    a. a route along which electrical current moves

b. a test for the intensity of electrical current

c. a formula for computing the amount of electricity

❏ THE INDEX

An index is an alphabetical list of topics and key terms discussed in a book, along with the page numbers where they appear. Turn to the Table of Contents in your *Knowledge Base,* and look up the page number of the Index. You will see that it's at the end of the book.

Look at the first page of the Index. As you can see, it has more detailed listings than the Table of Contents. Figure 2-3 shows a portion of the Index.

Computers, 7, 34-41
  circuit boards, 35-41, 74-76
  in function testing, 88, 90,
    91
  hardware, 36-40
  software, 40-41
  understanding, 35
	working with, 8-9
	Conductors, 34, 107
	  wire as, 68-69
	Connecting wire, 72-73
	Contracts, maintenance,
	  48-49
	Current (I), 24
		Customer relations, 94-95
		
		Data, 35, 39
		Design engineers, 10-11, 17
		Digital display, 81
		Digital equipment, 35
		Digits, 81

Figure 2-3

"Computer" is the main entry, or main listing. Subentries are words or terms that relate to the main entry. In this case, the subentries are the items listed under "Computer," such as "software." Subentries are listed alphabetically below the main entry, with the page numbers on which they can be found.

SELF-CHECK 2-5

Directions: *Use the Index in the* Knowledge Base *to answer the following questions.*

1. What page(s) contain information about resistors? _____

2. How many subentries are there under "Electronics"? _____

3. What is the main entry directly before "Ohmmeter"? _____

4. List the subentries under "Testers."

   _____

   _____

   _____

5. What pages discuss the topic "Circuits"? _____

6. In how many places in the *Knowledge Base* is the term *bytes* discussed? _____

Exercises

THE TABLE OF CONTENTS

1. On what page does Chapter 8 start? _____

2. In what chapter will you find the topic "Getting the Parts Together"?
   _____

3. How many topics, subtopics, and sub-subtopics are there in Chapter 4? _____

4. What section in Chapter 4 contains information about computer software? _____

5. On what page does the subtopic "Computers" begin? _____

THE LIST OF FIGURES

1. How many figures are there in Chapter 3? _____

2. How many figures are there in Chapter 9? _____

3. On what page is Figure 3-3 located? _____

4. What is the title of Figure 3-3? _____

   _____

5. On what page is Figure 8-2 located? _____

6. What is the title of Figure 8-2? _____

7. In what chapter do you find a figure that shows a computer showroom?

   _____

8. What is the number of the figure showing a work order form? ____

   _____

9. Turn to page 29 and find Figure 3-7.

   a. What is the caption for the figure? _____

      _____

   b. What is in the figure? _____

      _____

      _____

c. Draw two of the symbols in the figure and tell what they mean?

10. Turn to page 36 and find Figure 4-2.

    a. What is the caption for the figure? _____

    _____

    b. What is in the figure? _____

    _____

THE GLOSSARY

1. Use the Glossary in the *Knowledge Base* to write the definitions for the following terms:

    a. **data** _____

    _____

    b. **ground** _____

    _____

    _____

    c. **memory** _____

    _____

2. Use the Glossary to answer the following true or false questions.

    Circle *T* for true or *F* for false.

    a. T F A microchip can hold a lot of information because it is so large.

    b. T F A neutron is larger than an atom.

    c. T F A computer program helps to run a computer.

    d. T F A soldered joint always involves melting plastic.

THE INDEX

1. On what page or pages will you find information about each of the following topics:

   a. Diodes _____

   b. Inventory report_____

   c. Memory _____

   d. Bits _____

   e. Components _____

2. For each of the main entries listed, write the subentries:

   a. Meters

      _____

      _____

      _____

      _____

   b. Sales

      _____

P A R T

3

Reading to Learn

USING PQ3R

In Part 1, you learned the difference between *reading to do* and *reading to learn*. Then, in Part 2, you learned and practiced some reading-to-do tasks. Now, in Part 3, you will practice reading to learn.

When your goal is to master information, you are reading to learn. When you are reading to learn, you are an *active* reader. An active reader thinks *before* reading, *during* reading, and *after* reading. To learn to be an active reader, you will use a proven five-step process called "PQ3R":

To be an active reader, do:

P = Preview Before You Read

Q = Question

R = Read During Reading

R = Recode

R = Review After You Read

❏ *PQ3R:* PREVIEW

The first step in reading to learn is to preview the chapter or section you are about to read. When you preview, you skim the material quickly, reading the topic headings and looking at any illustrations, charts, or tables.

> In the office area, the receptionist keeps track of office supplies, such as envelopes, printed forms, notebooks, and pens. For those kinds of supplies, an exact *inventory system* is not needed. If the department ran out of pens, they could purchase them the same day. They would not have to stop working.
>
> In the manufacturing department, Benjamin has a very exact inventory system. You cannot just go and buy printed circuit boards with exact specifications. They have to be ordered. There are many items, such as housings, that have to be made by other manufacturers before Benjamin can receive them.
>
> Some of the items used by manufacturing can be bought at a local hardware store. It is not necessary to keep track of the exact number of screws-in house. However, Benjamin must keep track of a lot of items in his inventory so that he knows how many have been used.
>
> **Inventory Control**
>
> Keeping the right amount of supplies or parts on hand is known as *inventory control*. Managers need to know when to order inventory and how much to order.
>
> **When to Order**
>
> How does Benjamin know when to order manufacturing supplies? He does not want to order an item when he has plenty on hand. That wastes storage space. It also uses company money too far in advance of when an item is needed. In most companies, cash flow, or the availability of money, is usually a big concern. All the managers have been told to keep their budgets as small as possible.
>
> But, if Benjamin waits too long, he may run out of an item. That would waste expensive worker manufacturing time. One of the main tasks of a person in charge of inventory control is to decide when it is time to order an item.
>
> To decide when to order an item, you need certain facts. You need to know how fast your office uses up the item you

Figure 3-1

For example, as you skim the pages of Chapter 1 of your *Electricity and Electronics Technology Knowledge Base,* you might see the material shown in Figure 3-1. Note that the topic headings are set off from the text. Topic headings are like road signs; they tell you what's coming up. There are three kinds of headings in the *Knowledge Base—main headings, subheadings,* and *sub-subheadings.* These guide you from topic to topic in the material that you are reading. Notice that the main headings are in capital letters and are larger than the subheadings. The subheadings are underlined. Later, you will also see sub-subheadings that are not underlined and are slightly smaller than the subheadings.

SELF-CHECK 3-1

Directions: *Turn to Chapter 1 of the* Knowledge Base, *"Electricity and Electronics," and complete the following exercise.*

1. Write all the topic headings in Chapter 1. Write the main headings at the left margin. Indent the subheadings a few spaces.

_____

_____

_____

_____

_____

_____

_____

_____

_____

_____

2. How many main topics are there in Chapter 1? _____

3. How many subtopics are there (include *all* subheadings)? _____

4. How many figures are there in Chapter 1? _____

❏ PQ3R: QUESTION

After you preview Chapter 1, "Electricity and Electronics," ask yourself, "What do I already know about this topic?" This question will call to mind the information you already have in your brain, in your knowledge base. Do the same with each main heading and subheading in the chapter or section—ask yourself what you know about each topic. These questions will help you to focus "prior knowledge" on what you are about to read.

For example, look at page 8 in the *Knowledge Base.* When you see the subheading "Working With Computers," ask yourself, "What do I know about working with computers?" "What kind of computers have I seen?" As you ask yourself such questions, you prepare to learn more about each topic by recalling your prior knowledge.

SELF-CHECK 3-2

Directions: *Listed below are three subheadings from Chapter 1 of the* Knowledge Base. *For each subheading, ask yourself what you know about that topic. Then write the information in the space provided.*

1. Working With Computers

   _____

   _____

2. Working in the Energy Industry

   _____

   _____

3. What Is Electronics

   _____

   _____

❏ PQ3*R*: READ

You have previewed Chapter 1 so that you know which topics it covers. You have asked yourself questions so that you can relate the topics to your prior knowledge, or what you already know about each topic. Now you can actively begin to read.

Note the word *actively.* To make sure that you are reading actively, you must:

1. Underline key words as you read. In many books, some of the key words are already emphasized for you—for example, the words may be in **boldface,** in *italics,* or in CAPITAL letters. (As you previewed the chapter, you probably noticed that the key words about electricity and electronics in the *Knowledge Base* are in boldface. These bold-faced words are defined in the Glossary at the end of the book.)
2. Think about the questions you asked yourself in the "Question" step. How do your answers relate to the material you are about to read?

SELF-CHECK 3-3

Directions: *Read the section in Chapter 1 called "Working in Electricity and Electronics," including all of its subsections, starting on page 4. When you finish, close your book and underline the key words in the following paragraph. As you underline, think about whether the words are familiar— do you have prior knowledge of these terms?*

Almost everything we do in the world around us involves the use of electricity. Workers in electricity learn to make, install, or repair electrical circuits or machines. They keep power plants running. Electricity is the basic form of energy used in homes and businesses. Equipment that operates by the flow of electric charges is called electronic equipment. Electronics is the industry that makes, installs, and repairs electronic equipment.

As you completed Self-Check 3-3, you were reading *actively*. The goal of reading to learn is to understand what the author is saying and to remember it later on. The first step toward understanding is to grasp the main idea. This, after all, tells you what the author wants to say.

The *main idea* is the most important point in a paragraph or an article. The sentence that contains the core of the main idea is called the *topic sentence*. It is often the first sentence in the paragraph and is followed by details that support, explain, or describe the point. But the topic sentence is not always the first sentence; it may appear anywhere in the paragraph. So, most paragraphs have two basic parts: the *topic sentence* and *supporting details*.

Look at the following paragraph. The first sentence is the topic sentence here. Do you see how it clearly states the main idea?

Jobs involved with electricity and electronics are available in most industries. Some common industrial jobs available for electrical technicians are in power plants, manufacturing firms, and construction. Electronics technicians can work anywhere that electronic equipment is repaired, built, or serviced.

The topic sentence tells you that jobs involved with electricity and electronics are available in most industries. Then the supporting details follow:

1. Some common industrial jobs available for electrical technicians are in power plants, manufacturing firms, and construction.
2. Electronics technicians can work anywhere that electronic equipment is repaired, built or serviced.

These details support the main idea.

Now read the following example to see how a topic sentence can be placed at the end of a paragraph:

In construction, electricians need assistants to help with wiring. In power plants, technicians assist electrical engineers. In manufacturing, technicians perform many tasks. Electrical technicians are in great demand.

The topic sentence tells you that electrical technicians are in great demand. The rest of the paragraph tells you where they are in demand.

SELF-CHECK 3-4

Directions: Read the paragraphs in the Knowledge Base *that are indicated below. Then write the topic sentence and one or two supporting details for each paragraph.*

1. **Paragraph 1 under "Working With Computers" on page 8.**

Topic Sentence: _____

_____

Supporting Details: _____

_____

_____

2. **Paragraph 1 under "Professional Careers" on page 10.**

Topic Sentence: _____

_____

Supporting Details: _____

_____

❏ PQ3*R*: RECODE

The goal of previewing, questioning, and reading is, of course, to remember and use the information you read. Sometimes, though, you will forget the information you've read—that's natural. To help yourself remember what you read, it is important for you to *recode* information immediately after reading.

To *recode* means to express the information in another way. For example, you can recode material by putting it in your own words. This process is called *paraphrasing*. Another way to recode is to make a chart of the information or even to draw a picture. Each of these recoding activities—paraphrasing, making charts, drawing pictures—is covered in this book. Let's begin with paraphrasing.

PARAPHRASING Suppose you repeat a paragraph exactly as you read it in a book. That doesn't mean you *understand* what you're saying. On the other hand, expressing an idea *in your own words* does show understanding. If you did not understand the idea, you would not be able to paraphrase it.

To paraphrase a paragraph, (1) identify the topic sentence, which will tell you the main idea. Then (2) identify the supporting details. And finally, (3) try expressing the main idea and the supporting details *in your own words*, in words that feel natural to you.

Before you try paraphrasing, compare the following paragraph with the suggested paraphrase below it.

Electricity can be dangerous. Workers must understand how it works. They must also know all the safety rules. Students in a technician training course learn the basics of electricity. They also learn how it flows and how it can be dangerous.

Possible Paraphrase:

Workers have to understand electricity because it is dangerous. There are safety rules for dealing with electricity. Students learn how electricity works and why it is dangerous when they are training to be technicians.

Your paraphrase will be different because you will use *your own words*. As you can see, paraphrasing is an excellent technique for recoding. The paraphrasing exercises that follow will help you to use this recoding tool to remember what you read.

SELF-CHECK 3-5

Directions: Read the paragraphs indicated below. Then write a paraphrase of each paragraph.

1. **Paragraph 1 under "Working in Electricity and Electronics on page 4."** _____

   _____

   _____

   _____

   _____

2. **Paragraph 2 under "Working With Computers" on pages 8 and 9.** _____

   _____

   _____

   _____

❏ PQ3*R*: REVIEW

The final step is to review the material you have read. *Review* means to take another look at, or go over again. There are several effective ways to review what you have read:

1. *List the key points.* Write a list of all the main ideas in the material you have read. Be sure to look at the topic sentences as you develop your list.

2. *Write a summary.* A summary also includes the major points in the chapter or article, but it is not written in list form. Instead, the summary is in paragraph form. Again, be sure to look at all the topic sentences as you develop your summary.

3. *Make a list of the key terms.* In some cases, making this list may be the most helpful way to review what you have just read. By highlighting key terms, you will be reminded of main points.

4. *Skim the chapter again.* Repeating the preview process is another effective way to remember what you have read.

Which technique you use will depend on the type of material you are reading. In any case, you will remember more of what you read when you take time to review it.

SELF-CHECK 3-6

Directions: *Complete the following exercises.*

1. Write five of the key points in Chapter 1._____

_____

_____

_____

_____

_____

_____

_____

2. Write the key terms used in Chapter 1. _____

_____

_____

_____

_____

3. Write a brief summary—no more than two paragraphs long—of
    Chapter 1._____

_____

_____

_____

_____

_____

_____

_____

Practicing PQ3R With Chapter 2

Read Chapter 2 in the *Knowledge Base.* Use the PQ3R method in the
exercises that follow.

PREVIEW

1. What is the title of the chapter?

    _____

2. List the major section headings in Chapter 2.

    _____

    _____

3. List the figures in Chapter 2 by number, and write each figure caption.

    _____

    _____

    _____

    _____

    _____

QUESTION

1. Here is the title of Chapter 2 stated as a question:

    What is it like to work in electricity and electronics? Think about the question. Try to answer the question based on what you already know.

    _____

    _____

    _____

2. Change the two major section headings of Chapter 2 into questions.

    _____

    _____

3. Answer the questions you wrote in Exercise 2 based on what you already know.

    _____

    _____

    _____

    _____

READ

Read the section about the office area on pages 14 through 19 of the *Knowledge Base*. Then complete the following exercise.

1. Turn back to pages 14 and 15, and read the subsection called "Bookkeeping" again. Then close the book, and fill in the blanks in the paragraph below.

> The bookkeeper makes up the (a)_____ checks. Sal looks at a payroll (b)_____ to figure how much to pay each person. He checks the hours that each worker put in on their (c)____ _____. The workers (d)_____ their hours on the time cards. Sal's computer has a (e)_____ that figures and subtracts the taxes and prints the checks.

2. Read the following paragraph, and underline the key words.

> The inventory supervisor has a system for keeping track of inventory. All items to be shipped have a bar code. The bar code is read by an electronic device. The information goes to the supervisor's computer. The inventory system is just one of a number of systems for organizing work at Electroserve.

3. Turn to page 17, and read the fourth paragraph under "Engineering and Design." Identify the topic sentence and list the supporting details.

   Topic Sentence: _____

   _____

   Supporting Details: _____

   _____

   _____

4. Paraphrase the paragraph you just read for Exercise 3.

   _____

   _____

   _____

   _____

5. Turn to pages 19 and 20 in the *Knowledge Base*. Read the third paragraph under the heading "Managers." For that paragraph, list the topic sentence and supporting details.

   Topic Sentence: _____

   _____

Supporting Details: _____

_____

_____

_____

RECODE

1. Reread the first three paragraphs under the subheading "Inventory Department" on page 15. Paraphrase the main idea of each paragraph.

    a. **Paraphrase of Paragraph 1:** _____

    _____

    _____

    _____

    b. **Paraphrase of Paragraph 2:** _____

    _____

    _____

    c. **Paraphrase of Paragraph 3:** _____

    _____

    _____

2. Turn to page 17 of the *Knowledge Base,* and read the paragraph under the subheading "Sales." Paraphrase the main idea in the paragraph.

    _____

    _____

    _____

REVIEW

Now that you have read Chapter 2, do the following review activity.

1. List the major section headings in Chapter 2 and the key points covered in each section. Use a separate sheet of paper.

Practicing PQ3R With Chapter 3

Read Chapter 3 in the *Knowledge Base* using the PQ3R method.

PREVIEW

1. What is the title of the chapter?

    _____

2. List the major section headings in Chapter 3.

_____

_____

3. List the subsections under the first main heading.

_____

_____

_____

_____

4. List the figures in Chapter 3 by number, and write a short summary of each figure caption.

_____

_____

_____

_____

_____

_____

_____

_____

_____

QUESTION

1. Change the title of the chapter into a question.

_____

2. Think about the question you have written in Exercise 1. Try to answer the question based on what you already know.

_____

_____

_____

_____

3. Change the first major section heading into a question.

_____

4. Ask yourself what you know about the topic and how you might answer this question. Write your answer in the space provided.

_____

_____

_____

_____

5. Change the subheading on page 26 into a question.

_____

6. Ask yourself what you know about this topic, and write your answer in the space provided.

_____

_____

_____

_____

7. Look at Figure 3-4 on page 26. What is pictured in the figure? How would you use what is shown in the figure?

_____

_____

READ

1. Read the following paragraph, and underline the key words.

Electricity is energy. It is energy that comes from the movement of tiny particles called electrons. Everything—from air to wood—is made up of atoms. Even people are made up of atoms. Electrons move inside atoms. Also moving inside atoms are protons and neutrons.

2. Turn to page 24 in the *Knowledge Base,* and read the four paragraphs under the subheading "Current." For each paragraph in the subsection, write the topic sentence and list supporting details in the space provided.

Paragraph 1

Topic Sentence: _____

_____

Supporting Details: _____

_____

_____

Paragraph 2

Topic Sentence: _____

_____

Supporting Details: _____

_____

_____

Paragraph 3

Topic Sentence: _____

_____

Supporting Details: _____

_____

_____

Paragraph 4

Topic Sentence: _____

_____

Supporting Details: _____

_____

_____

3. Turn to page 24 in the *Knowledge Base*. For the two paragraphs in the subsection called "Static Electricity," write the topic sentence and supporting details.

Paragraph 1

Topic Sentence: _____

_____

Supporting Details: _____

_____

_____

_____

_____

Paragraph 2

Topic Sentence: _____

_____

Supporting Details: _____

_____

_____

4. Turn to pages 24 and 25 of the *Knowledge Base*. For the first three paragraphs in the subsection called "Energy and Power," write the topic sentence and supporting details.

Paragraph 1

Topic Sentence: _____

_____

Supporting Details: _____

_____

_____
_____
_____

Paragraph 2

Topic Sentence: _____

_____

Supporting Details: _____

_____

Paragraph 3

Topic Sentence: _____

_____

Supporting Detail: _____

_____

5. Turn to pages 26 and 27 in the *Knowledge Base,* and find the subsection called "Testing." For the first paragraph in the section, write the topic sentence and supporting details.

Topic Sentence: _____

_____

Supporting Details: _____

_____

_____

_____

_____

RECODE

1. Turn to pages 25 and 26 in the *Knowledge Base,* and reread the first three paragraphs in the section called "Electrical Repair." Write a one-paragraph paraphrase of all the information in these paragraphs.

_____

_____

_____

_____

_____

_____

2. Turn to page 29 in the *Knowledge Base,* and read the first three paragraphs under the subheading "Using Circuit Diagrams." Paraphrase each of the three paragraphs in the space provided.

a. **Paraphrase of Paragraph 1:**

_____

_____

_____

b. **Paraphrase of Paragraph 2:**

_____

_____

c. **Paraphrase of Paragraph 3:**

_____

_____

REVIEW

1. Write a two-paragraph summary of Chapter 3 on a separate sheet of paper. Recall that a chapter summary is one or more paragraphs that present the main ideas of a chapter. The first paragraph should cover the information in the section called "Electricity." The second paragraph should summarize the section "Electrical Repair."

2. Create a list of the key boldface terms in Chapter 3 on a separate sheet of paper. Define each one.

Review Your Knowledge

The following questions can be answered using the material you read in Chapters 1, 2, and 3 of the *Knowledge Base.* Without looking at the *Knowledge Base,* try to answer each of the questions.

CHAPTER 1

1. What is electricity? _____

_____

2. What is electronics? _____

_____

3. What is one of the largest industries in the world? _____

4. Name two important parts of the electronics industry? _____

_____

Circle the letter of the correct answer.

5. Your major job is to repair electronic devices. You got your training in a technical school. You specialize in repairing computers. You are:

    a. an engineer

    b. a designer

    c. an electronics technician

    d. an electrical technician

6. Mary works on programs at a computer service company. She has had good training. She is:

    a. a salesperson

    b. an apprentice

    c. a programmer

    d. a testing technician

Circle *T* for true or *F* for false.

7. T F All electrical circuits have computers.

8. T F Electronic equipment operates by the flow of electric charges.

CHAPTER 2

1. What is an inventory? _____

   _____

2. What is a bar code? _____

   _____

3. What is a circuit drawing? _____

   _____

4. What is a system? _____

   _____

5. Who does the planning for the company? _____

   _____

Circle the letter of the correct answer.

6. A circuit drawing is:

    a. designed by an engineer

    b. shows how electrical circuits will be connected

    c. made up for most new electrical and electronic products

    d. all of the above

7. Managers:

    a. sell all the products

b. oversee all the departments of a company

c. are responsible for designing circuits

d. all of the above

Circle _T_ for true or _F_ for false.

8. T F Electrical symbols are a kind of shorthand.

9. T F Each worker usually has his or her own system.

CHAPTER 3

1. What is an electron? _____

   _____

2. What is an electric charge? _____

   _____

3. What is a free electron? _____

   _____

4. What is a short circuit?_____

   _____

5. What is current measured in?_____

Circle the letter of the correct answer.

6. Energy is:

   a. the capacity to do work

   b. what you use when turning on a stove

   c. what you use when swinging a bat

   d. all of the above

7. Troubleshooting is a process that helps a technician:

   a. find out how the company's system works

   b. learn how to assemble products

   c. find the source of a problem with a product

   d. all of the above

Circle _T_ for true or _F_ for false.

8. T F Resistance is the quality that allows the electricity to flow freely.

9. T F Soldering is the joining together of two parts.

P A R T

4

Reading to Learn

MAKING MIND MAPS AND OUTLINES

In Part 3 you learned that one way to remember information that you have just read is to recode it. And one way to recode material is to paraphrase the main ideas—that is, take what you have read and put it into your own words.

❏ MIND MAPS

Another way to recode information is to make a mind map. In some ways, a mind map is like a map of a place. Think about what you would do if you were asked where Texas is. You would probably picture a map of the United States in your mind. Then you could look at your mind map to see how and where all the states fit together.

When you make a mind map, you create a picture in your mind of the main idea and supporting details. This picture helps you see, and recall later, how ideas fit together. For example, suppose you have to buy groceries but you forgot to make a list of what you need. You might picture in your mind your local supermarket or grocery store and what products are in each aisle. Then you could go from aisle to aisle in your head, and write items down under categories, such as "Dairy" (milk, eggs, juice); "Produce" (lettuce, apples); "Baking" (flour, sugar); and so on. A mind map of this information would look like Figure 4-1.

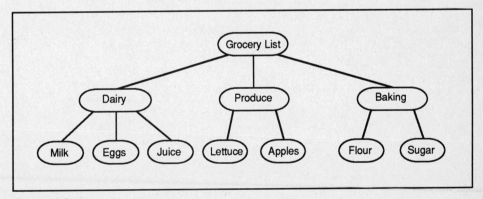

Figure 4-1

You can do the same thing with information that you read and want to remember. You learned in Chapter 2, for example, how work is supervised at a construction site. You learned about the job of general contractor and whom he or she supervises. A mind map of this information would look like Figure 4-2.

You can do the same thing with information that you read and want to remember. You learned in Chapter 3, for example, what is inside of an atom. A mind map of this information would look like Figure 4-2.

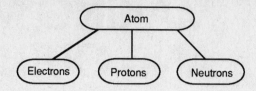

Figure 4-2

SELF-CHECK 4-1

Directions: *Turn to page 24 in the* Knowledge Base, *and read the first paragraph in the subsection entitled "Energy and Power." A mind map for this paragraph has been started for you in Figure 4-3. To finish it, you need to do the following:*

1. Find the three types of energy, and write them in the blank circles beneath the top circle.

2. Draw lines connecting the top circle to those immediately underneath.

3. Write details that support the categories in the circles beneath them.

4. Draw lines from the category circles to the supporting detail circles.

5. Continue adding levels of circles, if necessary, until all of the key information is shown in your mind map.

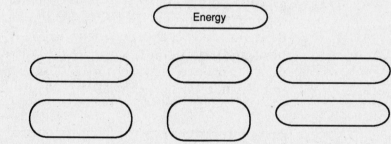

Figure 4-3

Generally, the longer the selection you are mapping, the more levels of circles your mind map will have. A mind map for a few paragraphs is much simpler than one for a whole chapter.

SELF-CHECK 4-2

Directions: *Turn to page 29 in the* Knowledge Base, *and read the first three paragraphs in the subsection called "Using Circuit Diagrams." Make a mind map of those paragraphs by putting the right information in the circles below.*

Part 4: Making Mind Maps and Outlines

SELF-CHECK 4-3

Directions: *Turn to pages 14 and 15 in the* Knowledge Base, *and read the subsection called "Bookkeeping." Create a mind map that shows how the bookkeeper figures out the payroll.*

❏ OUTLINES

Like a mind map, an outline is a way to recode information. Instead of circles connected by lines, however, letters and numbers show how main ideas and supporting details relate to each other. In an outline, the following symbols are used:

❏ Roman numerals (*I, II, III, IV, V, VI, VII, VIII, IX, X,* and so on) identify the main ideas.

❏ Capital letters (*A, B, C, D,* and so on) identify subtopics that are part of the main idea.

❏ Arabic numbers (*1, 2, 3, 4,* and so on) identify details that support subtopics.

❏ Lowercase letters (*a, b, c, d,* and so on) identify minor details.

All of these symbols are set up so that supporting details are indented under more important points. For example:

I. Main Idea
   A. Subtopic
      1. Supporting detail
      2. Supporting detail
         a. Minor supporting detail
         b. Minor supporting detail
   B. Subtopic
      1. Supporting detail
      2. Supporting detail
II. Main Idea
   A. Subtopic
   B. Subtopic
      1. Supporting detail
      2. Supporting detail
   C. Subtopic

The following passage is based on material from Chapter 1 in the *Knowledge Base*. After the passage, you'll find the same information in outline form. Notice that you do not have to use the exact words from a passage when presenting the information in outline form. In other words, when you make an outline, you often paraphrase.

> A manufacturing company generally has six major divisions. The office area takes care of payroll, billing, and filing. The repair areas take care of warranties, customer complaints, and repair. The manufacturing division makes the products and finishes the parts of the products. The assembly division puts products together. In that division, clerks put together the kits for assembling. The testing division tests products and uses testers.

I. Manufacturing Company
   A. Office area
      1. Payroll
      2. Billing
      3. Filing
   B. Repair Area
      1. Warranties
      2. Customer complaints
      3. Repair
   C. Manufacturing Division
      1. Makes products
      2. Finishes product parts
   D. Assembly Division
      1. Puts products together
      2. Makes kits for assembly
   E. Testing Division
      1. Tests products
      2. Uses testers
II. (Next Main Idea)

Please note that, for every level of an outline, you should have at least two items. Therefore, if you label an item "A," you must have at least one more item (labeled "B") at the same level.

SELF-CHECK 4-4

Directions: Turn to page 7 in the Knowledge Base, *and read the first page in the section called "Jobs in Electricity and Electronics." Next, look at the following outline for the first part of what you just read. It identifies the main idea next to roman numeral I. It also identifies the first topic of the main idea next to the letter A and the three details that support topic A. Continue the outline by writing the next main topic beside the letter B, then writing supporting details.*

I. Jobs in Electricity and Electronics

    A. Electrical Technician

        1. Electrician's assistant

        2. Power plant worker

        3. Manufacturing technician

    B. _____

        1. _____

        2. _____

II. (Next Main Idea)

SELF-CHECK 4-5

Directions: Read the material in the Knowledge Base *beginning with the section called "Electricity" on page 22. (Stop when you get to the next section head, "Electrical Repair.") Based on your reading, create an outline for this material on a separate sheet of paper.*

Practicing PQ3R With Chapter 4

Read Chapter 4 in the *Knowledge Base*. Use the PQ3R method in the exercises that follow.

PREVIEW

1. What is the title of the chapter? _____

   _____

2. List the major section headings in Chapter 4.

   _____

   _____

3. List the subtopics for the first major section.

_____

_____

_____

_____

_____

4. List the figures in Chapter 4 by number, and write each figure caption. Shorten any long captions to a four- or five-word summary.

_____

_____

_____

_____

_____

_____

_____

_____

QUESTION

1. Change the title of the chapter into a question.

_____

2. Think about the question you have written in Exercise 1. Try to answer the question based on what you already know.

_____

_____

_____

3. Change the first major section heading into a question.

_____

4. Ask yourself what you know about the topic and how you might answer this question. Write your answer in the space provided.

_____

_____

_____

_____

_____

_____

5. Change the second major section heading into a question.

    _____

6. Ask yourself what you know about this topic, and write your answer
    below.

    _____

    _____

    _____

    _____

7. Look at Figure 4-8. What is pictured in the figure? Name several
    electronic devices that might have this part.

    _____

    _____

    _____

READ

1. Read the following paragraph, and underline the key words.

The most important electronic product today is probably the computer. Computers are made up of two main elements—hardware and software. The hardware includes all the electronic circuits inside the central processing unit of the computer. It also includes the monitor, keyboard, power supply, and any other parts that you can see and touch. The software includes programs for running the computer.

---

2. Turn to page 32 find the section "Electronics." For the first two
    paragraphs in the section, list the topic sentence and supporting
    details in the space provided.

    Paragraph 1

    Topic Sentence: _____

    _____

    Supporting Details: _____

    _____

    _____

Paragraph 2

Topic Sentence: _____

_____

Supporting Details: _____

_____

_____

3. Turn to pages 36 and 37, and find the subsection "Computer Hardware." For the first four paragraphs in the subsection, list the topic sentence and supporting details in the space provided.

Paragraph 1

Topic Sentence: _____

_____

Supporting Details: _____

_____

Paragraph 2

Topic Sentence: _____

_____

Supporting Details: _____

_____

_____

_____

_____

Paragraph 3

Topic Sentence: _____

_____

Supporting Details: _____

_____

Paragraph 4

Topic Sentence: _____

_____

Supporting Details: _____

_____

RECODE

1. Reread the paragraphs in the subsection "Understanding Computers" on page 35. Using the topic sentence and supporting details, paraphrase each paragraph.

    a. **Paraphrase of Paragraph 1:**

    _____

    _____

    _____

    _____

    _____

    b. **Paraphrase of Paragraph 2:**

    _____

    _____

2. Turn to page 35 in the *Knowledge Base,* and find the subsection called "Circuit Boards." Paraphrase the information in the paragraph.

    Paraphrase:

    _____

    _____

    _____

    _____

3. Turn to pages 36 through 39 of the *Knowledge Base,* and find the subsection "Computer Hardware." Make a mind map of paragraphs 5 through 10 in this subsection.

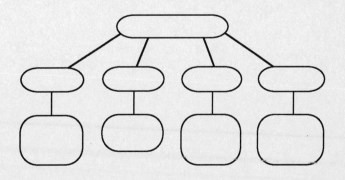

REVIEW

1. Write a two-paragraph summary of Chapter 4 on a separate sheet of paper. Recall that a chapter summary is one or more paragraphs that present the main ideas of a chapter. The first paragraph should summarize electronics. The second paragraph should summarize repairing electronic machines.

Practicing PQ3R With Chapter 5

Read Chapter 5 in the *Knowledge Base* using the PQ3R method.

PREVIEW

1. What is the title of the chapter:

   _____

2. List the major section headings in Chapter 5.

   _____
   _____
   _____
   _____
   _____

3. List the subsections under "Making the Product."

   _____
   _____

4. List the figures and figure captions in Chapter 5.

   _____
   _____
   _____
   _____
   _____
   _____
   _____
   _____
   _____

_____

_____

_____

QUESTION

1. Change the title of Chapter 5 into a question.

    _____

2. Think about the question you have written in Exercise 1. Try to answer the question based on what you already know.

    _____

    _____

    _____

    _____

3. Change the first major section heading into a question.

    _____

4. Ask yourself what you know about the topic and how you might answer this question. Write your answer in the space provided.

    _____

    _____

    _____

    _____

5. Change the second major section heading into a question.

    _____

6. Ask yourself what you know about this topic, and write your answer below.

    _____

    _____

    _____

    _____

7. Change the third major section heading into a question.

    _____

8. Ask yourself what you know about this topic, and write your answer below.

    _____

    _____

    _____

9. Look at Figure 5-1. What is pictured in the figure? If you have ever used such a machine, describe what it was like.

_____

_____

_____

READ

1. Read the following paragraph, and underline the key words.

The manufacturing at Electroserve involves several steps. If a product or one of its parts is to be made by the company, then workers on manufacturing machinery will do it. If, on the other hand, Electroserve is just assembling parts, such as housings, printed circuit boards, power supplies, and switches, then the assembly team will do the work.

2. Turn to the section "Filling Orders" on page 46. List the topic sentences and supporting details for the three paragraphs in that section.

Paragraph 1

Topic Sentence: _____

_____

Supporting Details: _____

_____

_____

Paragraph 2

Topic Sentence: _____

_____

Supporting Details: _____

_____

_____

Paragraph 3

Topic Sentence: _____

_____

Supporting Details: _____

_____

_____

_____

3. Turn to page 46 in the *Knowledge Base.* For the first three paragraphs in the section called "Planning," write the topic sentence and supporting details.

Paragraph 1

Topic Sentence: _____

_____

Supporting Detail: _____

_____

Paragraph 2

Topic Sentence: _____

_____

Supporting Detail: _____

_____

Paragraph 3

Topic Sentence: _____

_____

Supporting Details: _____

_____

_____

4. Turn to pages 46 and 47 in the *Knowledge Base,* and find the subsection called "Making Purchases." For the first paragraph in that subsection, write the topic sentence and supporting details.

Topic Sentence: _____

_____

Supporting Details: _____

_____

_____

RECODE

1. Read the three paragraphs in the subsection on pages 50 and 51 called "When to Order." Write a paraphrase of each paragraph.

   a. **Paraphrase of Paragraph 1:**

   _____

_____

_____

   b. **Paraphrase of Paragraph 2:**

_____

_____

   c. **Paraphrase of Paragraph 3:**

_____

_____

_____

2. Turn to page 47 in the *Knowledge Base,* and find the subsection called "Major Purchases." Make a mind map of the second paragraph in this section.

REVIEW

1. Write a five-paragraph summary of Chapter 5 on a separate sheet of paper. Recall that a chapter summary is one or more paragraphs that present the main ideas of a chapter. Each of the five paragraphs should summarize the material in one of the five major section heads.

2. Create a list of the key terms in Chapter 5 on a separate sheet of paper. Define each one.

Practicing PQ3R With Chapter 6

PREVIEW

1. What is the title of Chapter 6? _____

_____

2. List all of the major topic headings in Chapter 6.

_____

_____

3. List all the subtopics and sub-subtopics under the first major topic heading in Chapter 6.

_____

_____

_____

_____

_____

_____

4. List the figures and figure captions in Chapter 6.

_____

_____

_____

_____

_____

_____

_____

_____

_____

_____

_____

_____

_____

QUESTION

1. In the space provided, write what you already know about each of the major topic headings in Chapter 6.

a. _____

_____

_____

b. _____
_____
_____

READ

1. Turn to pages 64 through 66 in the *Knowledge Base*. Read the first three paragraphs in the section called "Getting the Parts Together." When you have finished, close the book and fill in the blanks in the following paragraph.

The assembly area has a supply room. The clerks put together (a)____ that contains all the parts needed to (b)_____ a product. Some parts such as a computer (c)_____ may be several feet wide. Others, such as circuit (d)_____, may be just a couple of inches wide.

2. Restate in your own words the main idea of the preceding paragraph.

_____
_____

3. Read the subsection called "Electrical Wire" on pages 69 through 72 of the *Knowledge Base*. For the first two paragraphs in this subsection, write the topic sentence in the space below.

Paragraph 1

Topic Sentence: _____

_____

Paragraph 2

Topic Sentence: _____

_____

4. Read the subsection in the *Knowledge Base* called "Electronic Wire" on pages 74 and 75. When you are finished, close your book and answer the following true-false questions. **(Circle *T* for true or *F* for false.)**

a. T F Electronic wire usually has many strands.

b. T F Printed circuit boards need a base that is a good insulator.

c. T F The components must not allow electricity to pass through them.

5. Turn to pages 69 through 72 in the *Knowledge Base*, and find the subsection entitled "Electrical Wire." Reread the first three paragraphs in that subsection. In the space below, restate in your own words the main idea for each paragraph.

   Paragraph 1

   Main Idea: _____

   _____

   Paragraph 2

   Main Idea: _____

   _____

   Paragraph 3

   Main Idea: _____

   _____

6. Reread the entire subsection called "Electrical Wire," on pages 69 through 72 of the *Knowledge Base*. When you have finished, close your book and fill in the blanks in the following paragraph.

Solid wire does not (a)_____ easily. Wire that needs to be bent is usually made of (b)_____ held together by a (c)_____. Groups of stranded wire are called (d)_____. Wiring needs to have an (e)_____ covering. Wires are conductors of electricity. Different conductors have different (f)_____.

---

7. Turn to pages 66 through 68 of the *Knowledge Base*, and read the subsection called "Assembling the Parts." In the space below, restate in your own words the main idea for each of the first three paragraphs in that section.

   Paragraph 1

   Main Idea: _____

   _____

   Paragraph 2

   Main Idea: _____

   _____

   Paragraph 3

   Main Idea: _____

   _____

8. Read the subsection called "Basic Wiring" on pages 68 and 69 of the *Knowledge Base*. When you have finished, close your book and fill in the blanks in the following paragraph.

Electrical wiring is the kind of wire that (a)_____ into an outlet in the wall. It also is used to conduct electricity inside some machines. Electronic wire allows (b)_____ to flow in a path "printed" on a (c)_____ _____. Good conductors, such as (d)_____ and (e)_____, are laid out on the board.

---

9. Read the subsection called "Electronic Wire" on pages 74 and 75 of the *Knowledge Base*. Close your book and answer the following true-false questions. **(Circle *T* for true or *F* for false.)**

  a. T F   A printed circuit board plugs into an outlet.

  b. T F   A good insulator, such as fiberglass, blocks the flow of electrons.

  c. T F   The wire on a printed circuit board allows current to flow to the various components.

RECODE

1. Turn to pages 66 through 68 in the *Knowledge Base*, and find the subsection called "Assembling the Parts." Draw a mind map for the information in that subsection.

2. Turn to pages 72 and 73 of the *Knowledge Base*, and create a mind map of the information in the subsection called "Connecting Wire."

REVIEW

1. Create a list of key words in Chapter 6. Define each one. Use a separate sheet of paper.

Review Your Knowledge

The following questions can be answered using the material you read in Chapters 4, 5, and 6. Without looking at the *Knowledge Base,* try to answer each question.

CHAPTER 4

1. What is a material that allows for the easy flow of electricity? ____

   _____

2. What is a chip? _____

   _____

3. How many bits are in a byte? _____

4. What is an integrated circuit? _____

   _____

5. Name four common types of components. _____

   _____

Circle the letter of the correct answer.

6. A resistor is:

    a. a component that connects to a printed circuit board

    b. a device that resists the flow of current

    c. a device used in electronic design

    d. all of the above

7. A computer program:

    a. instructs computers to perform tasks

    b. has at least six integrated circuit boards

    c. controls the temperature of the computer

    d. all of the above

Circle *T* for true or *F* for false.

8. T   F   Upgrading electronic equipment means changing it for the better.

9. T   F   A diode allows electricity to flow in two directions.

CHAPTER 5

1. What is a computer housing?: _____

    _____

2. What is the first stage of manufacturing?: _____

3. What is a warranty? _____

    _____

    _____

4. What is a maintenance contract? _____

    _____

    _____

Circle the letter of the correct answer.

5. Shelf life is:

    a. the length of time before an item sells

    b. the length of a shelf

    c. the length of time an item can stay on the shelf

    d. all of the above

6. Inventory control:

    a. helps companies know what they have in stock

    b. keeps track of supplies that must be ordered

    c. helps companies make sure parts are available

    d. all of the above

Circle *T* for true and *F* for false.

7. T   F   Unit price is the price per item.

8. T   F   *On back order* means that the company has too many in stock.

CHAPTER 6

1. What is a kit? _____

   _____

2. What is solid wire? _____

   _____

3. What is stranded wire? _____

   _____

4. What is the difference between a conductor and a resistor? _____

_____

_____

Circle the letter of the correct answer.

5. Resistance is determined by:

    a. the size of the wire

    b. the length of the wire

    c. the material used and its temperature

    d. all of the above

Circle *T* for true or *F* for false.

6. T F   Fiberglass is a good conductor.

7. T F   Electronic components may have switches that turn on or off as the current flows through them.

8. T F   Connecting a conductor to an insulator allows the electricity to flow freely.

9. T F   The *National Electrical Code* sets standards for using electricity.

10. T F   Soldering means taping wires together.

CHANGING TEXT TO PICTURES, TABLES, AND FLOWCHARTS

You have learned to recode information by paraphrasing and by making mind maps and outlines. Drawing a picture about what you've read is yet another way to recode material. Maybe you've heard the saying, "A picture is worth a thousand words." That saying is based on the belief that ideas are often easier to understand—and remember—when they are presented as a picture instead of in words.

For example, look at the picture of the manufacturing company in the front of the *Knowledge Base*. Because this picture is the first thing you see, it sets the scene for the whole book. When you finish the *Knowledge Base* and try to recapture the main points, the picture will provide you with a mental image of the work taking place at a manufacturing company.

❏ CHANGING TEXT TO PICTURES

You don't have to be an artist to be able to change text to pictures. To recode information in picture form, you first list the main ideas and supporting details. Then illustrate them in a way that has meaning for you. Later, when you need to recall the information, the picture you drew will help jog your memory about other details.

Turn to pages 69 and 70 of the *Knowledge Base,* and read the first three paragraphs of the subsection called "Electrical Wire." A picture of this information might look something like the one shown in Figure 5-1. Note that the key parts are labeled.

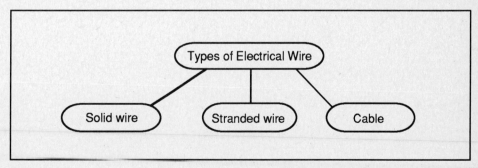

Figure 5-1

SELF-CHECK 5-1

Directions: *Now turn to page 22 in the* Knowledge Base, *and read the paragraph under the main heading "Electricity."*

1. Write the main idea and supporting details for the paragraph.

   Main Idea: _____

   _____

   Supporting Details: _____

   _____

   _____

   _____

   _____

2. In the space provided, recode the information about electricity as a picture. Remember to label each part of the picture.

❑ CHANGING TEXT TO TABLES

Some types of information lend themselves to recoding as tables. When you have groups of material, a table helps you find specific information quickly. And when you want to recall details, picturing the rows and columns of the table in your mind is a memory aid.

To create a table, you must first put the information in groups or categories. For example, if you were making a table that contained information about working in manufacturing, you might use categories such as "Area" and "Function." Then you decide on the best way to present the information. Sometimes, you will use labels only for the *columns* in the table. Sometimes, you will use labels for both *rows* and *columns*.

Turn to pages 43 through 46 of the *Knowledge Base*, and read the material on manufacturing. Below is a table that shows a different way to recode some of the information about areas in manufacturing and their function.

Manufacturing

Area or Division	Function
Planning	Plans and assigns work
Machining	Makes parts
Assembling	Puts together products
Testing	Tests parts and products

Each of the places where a row intersects with a column is called a cell. For example, the entry "Makes parts" is a cell. It is the cell where the column labeled "Function" intersects with the row labeled "Machining." Now that the material in the sections has been recoded in the form of a table, you can use it to find information quickly.

SELF-CHECK 5-2

Directions: *Turn to pages 47 through 49 in the* Knowledge Base. *Read the subsection called "Major Purchases." Recode the information within the table below.*

Major Purchases

Record of Purchase	Major Functions
Purchase information	
Instructions on use	
Warranties	
Maintenance contracts	

SELF-CHECK 5-3

Read the paragraph below. After you have finished reading, use the space provided to recode the information in the form of a table.

There are four major types of electronic components that go on circuit boards. They are resistors, transistors, diodes, and capacitors. They each have different purposes. A resistor blocks the flow of electricity. A transistor increases, changes, or switches electrical action. A diode allows current to flow in one direction only. A capacitor collects and stores electric charges.

❏ CHANGING TEXT TO FLOWCHARTS

A flowchart is a diagram that shows each step of a process or system. Recoding information in the form of a flowchart is helpful when you are trying to understand and remember the steps in a process or a series of events that lead to a specific result.

Flowcharts use connecting lines and special symbols, which are described below.

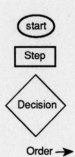

A *circle* indicates the beginning or end of a process or series.

A *box* contains one step in the process.

A *diamond* contains a question; it tells you a decision must be made.

An *arrow* shows the order of steps or events; it connects the other symbols.

In the two examples that follow, material is given in text form, and then it is recoded on flowcharts.

EXAMPLE 1

To dial a long-distance number direct, you first dial "1." Then you dial the area code followed by the seven-digit local number.

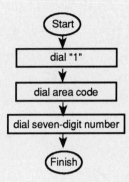

As you can see, the flowchart in Example 1 shows three steps. Below is a different kind of flowchart. It involves a decision.

EXAMPLE 2

When a technician works in electrical repair, certain basic steps help make the task easier. For example, the first item to check is the battery. If it is good, then the technician will go through a series of troubleshooting steps to find the problem and fix it. If the battery is not good, the technician will replace it.

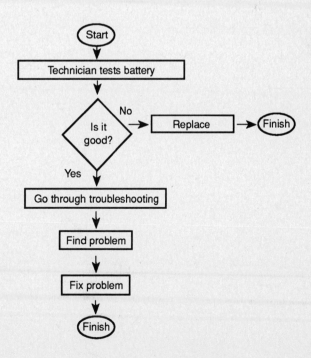

As you can see, when you use a decision box, you create two paths for the flowchart. In Example 2, if the technician finds that the battery is bad, he or she will replace it. On the other hand, if the battery is good, then the technician needs to follow a troubleshooting procedure to find the problem and fix it.

SELF-CHECK 5-4

Directions: *Turn to page 46 in the Knowledge Base, and read the section called "Filling Orders." Recode the information in the flowchart provided here.*

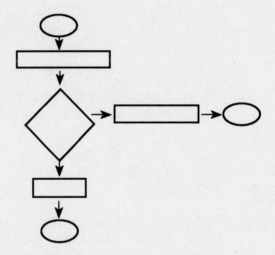

SELF-CHECK 5-5

Directions: *Turn to pages 53 and 54 in the Knowledge Base, and read the subsection called "Ordering Supplies." In the flowchart provided here, recode the information in that section.*

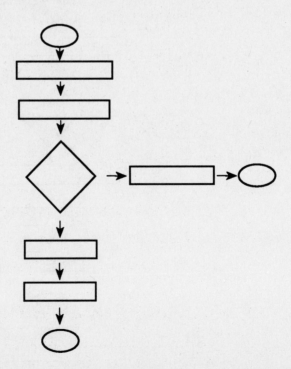

SELF-CHECK 5-6

Directions: *Read the following passage. In the space provided, draw a flowchart that represents the information in the passage.*

> The testing supervisor is checking the work of a new employee. The worker has finished testing five products. The supervisor is now going to retest the products and make sure that the results match those of the worker. If the results match, the worker will continue to test the products with less supervision. If the results do not match, the supervisor will spend more time training the worker until the worker understands the testing procedures.

Practicing PQ3R With Chapter 7

PREVIEW

1. What is the title of the chapter? _____

    _____

2. List the major topic headings in Chapter 7.

    _____

    _____

    _____

3. List the figures and figure captions in Chapter 7.

    _____

_____

_____

_____

_____

_____

_____

_____

_____

_____

_____

_____

_____

QUESTION

1. Ask yourself what you know about each of the three major topic headings in Chapter 7, and write your responses in the space provided.

   a. _____

   _____

   _____

   _____

   b. _____

   _____

   _____

   _____

   c. _____

   _____

   _____

   _____

READ

1. Turn to pages 79 and 80 in the *Knowledge Base*. Read the first three paragraphs in the section called "Testing Procedures." For each of the three paragraphs, restate in your own words the main idea.

Paragraph 1

Main Idea: _____

_____

Paragraph 2

Main Idea: _____

_____

Paragraph 3

Main Idea: _____

_____

2. Read the subsection called "Meters" on page 81. Identify the topic sentence and supporting details for each of the first two paragraphs.

Paragraph 1

Topic Sentence: _____

_____

Supporting Details: _____

_____

_____

_____

_____

Paragraph 2

Topic Sentence: _____

_____

Supporting Details: _____

_____

_____

_____

_____

_____

_____

3. Read the subsection called "Ammeter" on pages 82 and 83 of the *Knowledge Base*. Then close your book, and fill in the blanks in the following paragraph.

An ammeter measures (a)_____. An abbreviation for amperes is (b)____. An ampere is a measure of (c)_____ flow. DC or (d)_____ _____ is current that flows in one direction only. AC or (e)_____ _____ regularly changes its direction of flow.

RECODE

1. Turn to pages 83 and 84 in the *Knowledge Base*. Reread the subsection called "Voltmeter." Write a one-paragraph paraphrase of all the information in that section. _____

    _____

    _____

    _____

2. Turn to page 80 in the *Knowledge Base*. Restate in your own words the main idea for the first, second, and third paragraphs on that page.

    Paragraph 3

    Main Idea: _____

    _____

    Paragraph 4

    Main Idea: _____

    _____

    Paragraph 5

    Main Idea: _____

    _____

3. Make a mind map of the different kinds of meters described in the subsection "Meters" on pages 81 through 85.

4. Make a flowchart of the second paragraph under the subheading "Meters" on page 75.

5. On a separate sheet of paper, make an outline of Chapter 7.

REVIEW

1. Create a list of key terms in Chapter 7, using a separate sheet of paper. Then define each one.

Practicing PQ3R With Chapter 8

PREVIEW

1. List the section headings in Chapter 8.

2. How many figures are there in Chapter 8? _____

3. List the figures and figure captions in Chapter 8.

_____

_____

_____

_____

_____

_____

_____

_____

_____

QUESTION

1. Ask yourself what you know about the four section headings in Chapter 8. Write your response in the space provided.

a. _____

_____

_____

b. _____

_____

_____

c. _____

_____

_____

d. _____

_____

_____

READ

1. Turn to pages 95 and 96 in the *Knowledge Base*. Read the first two paragraphs under the subheading "Knowing the Rules of Safety." Identify the topic sentence in each paragraph.

Paragraph 1

Topic Sentence: _____

_____

Paragraph 2

Topic Sentence: _____

_____

2. Read the section called "Dealing With Customers" on pages 94 and 95 of the *Knowledge Base*. Then close your book and fill in the blanks in the following paragraph.

Good manners are always important in dealing with (a)_____. When a technician has an on-site service call, it is best to schedule an (b)_____ before going to the site. It is important not to interfere with (c)_____ that is taking place. Make sure to (d)_____ up whatever mess you make.

RECODE

1. Turn to pages 98 and 99 in the *Knowledge Base*, and reread the subsection called "Knowing What to Look For." Then create a mind map of the information in this subsection.

2. Read the subsection called "Fixing a Problem" on pages 99 and 100 of the *Knowledge Base*. Write a one-paragraph paraphrase of all the information in this subsection.

_____
_____
_____

3. Write an outline of Chapter 8.

_____
_____
_____
_____
_____
_____

_____

_____

_____

_____

_____

_____

_____

_____

_____

REVIEW

1. Pretend that you are an electrical technician going to a clothing store to fix a cash register. On a separate sheet of paper, list at least six steps that show how you would handle this job.

Practicing PQ3R With Chapter 9

PREVIEW

1. What is the title of Chapter 9? _____

_____

2. List the two major topic headings in Chapter 9.

_____

_____

3. List the figures and figure captions in Chapter 9.

_____

_____

_____

_____

_____

_____

_____

QUESTION

1. Ask yourself what you already know about each of the two main section headings in Chapter 9 of the *Knowledge Base*. Write what you know in the space below.

   a. _____
   _____
   _____

   b. _____
   _____
   _____

READ

1. Turn to pages 104 through 106 of the *Knowledge Base*. Read the subsection called "The Power of Electricity." In the space provided below, write a one-paragraph paraphrase of the main ideas in the first three paragraphs in that section.

   _____
   _____
   _____
   _____

2. Read the section called "Handling Electricity" on pages 106 through 110 of the *Knowledge Base*. When you have finished, close your book and fill in the blanks in the following paragraph.

Electricity is a major source of (a)_____. Electricity can only move through or along (b)_____. Technicians often use tools with a coated handle that will not (c)_____ electricity. Many machines need to be (d)_____ when connected to electricity.

---

3. Read the paragraph in the subsection called "Static Electricity" on page 106 of the *Knowledge Base*. In the space below, write the topic sentence and supporting details for that paragraph.

   Topic Sentence: _____

   _____

   Supporting Details: _____

RECODE

1. Turn to page 104 of the *Knowledge Base*. Read the paragraph under the main heading "Understanding Electricity." Write a paraphrase of that paragraph.

   _____

   _____

   _____

2. Reread pages 106 through 110 of the *Knowledge Base*. Draw a mind map of all the information in the "handling electricity" section.

3. Make an outline of the information in Chapter 9.

   _____

   _____

   _____

   _____

   _____

   _____

   _____

   _____

   _____

   _____

4. Turn to pages 107 and 108 in the *Knowledge Base*. Make a flowchart of the information on those pages about blocking and discharging electricity.

REVIEW

1. On a separate sheet of paper, create a list of key terms in Chapter 9. Define each one.

2. Write a summary paragraph for each of the two major sections in the chapter. Use a separate sheet of paper.

Review Your Knowledge

The following questions can be answered using the information you read in Chapters 7, 8, and 9. Without looking at the *Knowledge Base*, try to answer each question.

CHAPTER 7

1. What is a tester? _____

2. What is the difference between analog and digital? _____

    _____

    _____

3. What are the three common electrical testers? _____

_____

_____

_____

4. What is an ampere? _____

_____

Circle *T* for true or *F* for false.

5. T F Direct current alternates direction.

6. T F Alternating current regularly changes the direction of flow.

7. T F An ohm is a measure of resistance.

8. T F An oscilloscope is the same as a battery.

CHAPTER 8

1. What are five basic rules for service people to follow when dealing with customers? _____

_____

_____

_____

_____

_____

2. What is a circuit breaker box? _____

_____

3. Why does an electrician follow certain codes? _____

_____

4. Why do some tools have rubber or plastic handles? _____

_____

5. Why must a technician keep track of hours worked? _____

_____

Circle *T* for true or *F* for false.

6. T F It is okay to work on wires with the power supply on if you use insulated tools.

7. T F Technicians should schedule on-site appointments whenever possible.

8. T F The technician does an on-site check to make sure the equipment works at the site.

CHAPTER 9

1. What is electricity? _____

   _____

2. What is the world's major source of power? _____

   _____

3. What happens when electricity arcs? _____

   _____

4. Why do technicians discharge electricity from some devices? _____

   _____

Circle *T* for true or *F* for false.

5. T   F   Water does not conduct electricity.

6. T   F   Some articles of clothing can conduct electricity.

7. T   F   A grounded wire is safer than one without a ground.

Answer Key

SELF-CHECK 1-1

Answers will vary.

SELF-CHECK 1-2

1. Answers will vary.
2. Answers will vary.
3. Answers will vary.

SELF-CHECK 1-3

Answers will vary, but students should include the index, glossary, or list of figures.

SELF-CHECK 1-4

1. Reading to do
2. Reading to learn
3. Reading to learn
4. Reading to do
5. Reading to do
6. Reading to learn
7. Reading to learn
8. Reading to do
9. Reading to learn
10. Reading to learn

SELF-CHECK 1-5

1. Answers will vary.
2. Answers will vary.
3. Answers will vary.
4. Answers will vary.
5. Answers will vary.

SELF-CHECK 1-6

Answers will vary.

SELF-CHECK 1-7

1. Answers will vary.
2. Answers will vary.
3. Answers will vary.
4. Answers will vary.
5. Answers will vary.

SELF-CHECK 1-8

1. Answers will vary.
2. Answers will vary.
3. Answers will vary.
4. Answers will vary.
5. Answers will vary.

Answer Key

SELF-CHECK 2-1

1. 9

2. Assembling Electronic Products

3. 2

4. Getting the Parts Together

   Job Numbers

   Assembling the Parts

   Basic Wiring

   Electrical Wire

   Connecting Wire

   Electronic Wire

   Inserting Printed Circuit Boards

   Finishing the Product

5. page 13

6. Testers: Chapter 7

   Making Purchases: Chapter 5

7. Answers will vary, but students should say that it lists the topics covered in the book and gives the page number on which the discussion of each topic begins.

SELF-CHECK 2-2

1. 14

2. Figure 4-2

3. page 45

4. Chapter 6 and Chapter 7

5. Chapter 7

6. page 110

7. Answers will vary, but students should say that a list of figures helps them locate the chapter where the figure appears and the figure's placement within the chapter.

SELF-CHECK 2-3

1. a. married

   b. total hours; gross pay; FICA; FWT; Take-home pay

2. a. cash register pad

   b. 6

   c. Technician and supervisor

SELF-CHECK 2-4

1. c

2. b

3. a

SELF-CHECK 2-5

1. 37; 38

2. 2

3. office area

4. battery; meters; oscillosocopes

5. 4; 27

6. 1

EXERCISES

THE TABLE OF CONTENTS

1. page 93

2. Chapter 6

3. 8

4. Electronics

5. page 34

THE LIST OF FIGURES

1. 10

2. 7

3. page 25

4. Static electricity shown in the hair of a girl standing next to a static electricity generator.

5. page 96

6. A well-lighted menu board

7. Chapter 1

8. Figure 8-6

9. a. A circuit diagram showing symbols.

   b. Various circuits with symbols showing devices.

   c. Answers will vary.

10. a. A computer monitor.

    b. A monitor in use.

THE GLOSSARY

1. a. **data** Information in numerical form that is stored or processed in a computer.

   b. **ground** An electrical conductor attached to the earth. Also, to connect electricity to such a conductor. A grounded outlet is considered safe.

   c. **memory** The part of a computer where data can be stored for later use.

2. a. False

   b. False

   c. True

   d. False

THE INDEX

1. a. pages 37, 38, 39

   b. pages 53, 54

   c. page 35

   d. page 35

   e. pages 37, 75

2. a. Ammeter, multimeter, ohmmeter, voltmeter

   b. Opportunities in

Answer Key

SELF-CHECK 3-1

1. Working in Electricity and Electronics

   What Is Electricity?

   What Is Electronics?

   Jobs in Electricity and Electronics

   Electrical Technician

   Electronics Technician

   Working With Computers

   Working in the Energy Industry

   Professional Careers

   Technical Training

2. 3

3. 7

4. 6

SELF-CHECK 3-2

1. Answers will vary.

2. Answers will vary.

3. Answers will vary.

SELF-CHECK 3-3

Answers will vary. Terms should include *electricity, electrical circuits, electrical machines, power plants, energy, electric charges, electronics,* and *electronic equipment.*

SELF-CHECK 3-4

1. Topic Sentence: Electronics technicians can specialize in computers.

   Supporting Details: The manufacturers of computers employ technicians in the manufacturing process. Computer repair services employ trained technicians.

2. Topic Sentence: People who decide to go further with their electrical or electronic training have boundless opportunities.

   Supporting Details: The computer field keeps changing rapidly. Design engineers are always in demand.

SELF-CHECK 3-5

1. Possible Answer: Electricity is very important in the world. Almost every device we use, from lights to radios, runs on electricity. People who work with electricity learn how to fix, manufacture, and install electrical machines.

2. Possible Answer: Computer technicians can become data-entry people. They can also work on programs, the information that helps to run a computer.

SELF-CHECK 3-6

1. Possible Answers:

    Electricity is the basic form of energy used around the world. Electronic devices are operated by the flow of electric charges. Electrical technicians can work in a variety of jobs in many industries. Electronics technicians can also work in a variety of industries, especially those involving computers. Electricity is dangerous and requires careful handling.

2. Answers will vary. Terms should include *electricity, electrical, electrical circuits, electronics, electronic, electric, computers, programs,* and *testers.*

3. Answers will vary.

CHAPTER 2

PREVIEW

1. Working in Electricity and Electronics

2. The Office Area

    Managers

3. Figure 2-1 A payroll register.

    Figure 2-2 A bar code.

    Figure 2-3 An inventory report.

    Figure 2-4 A circuit drawing.

    Figure 2-5 A register pad used in a fast-food restaurant.

QUESTION

1. Answers will vary.

2. What is the office area?

    What does a manager do?

3. Answers will vary.

READ

1. a. payroll

    b. register

    c. time card

    d. punch

    e. program

2. Answers will vary. Terms should include *inventory*, *bar code*, *electronic device*, *computer*, and *system*.

3. Topic Sentence: Joan shows you some technical drawings.

   Supporting Details: These drawings show some basic designs. They show how the circuits will be connected. Figure 2-4 shows a drawing of a circuit.
   4. Possible Answer: Joan presents design drawings. These drawing are technical and show how the circuits will look. An example is in Figure 2-4.

5. Topic Sentence: Electroserve has been in business for 20 years.

   Supporting Details: During that time our business has changed greatly. We continue to serve our old clients. We supply them with electrical items, such as safety lights. But now, we mainly concentrate on electronic items, such as the drive-thru system that Joan is designing.

RECODE

1. Possible Answers:

   a. You meet Katy Arnold, the inventory supervisor. She was once an assembler and moved up to be a supervisor. When she studied electricity and electronics, she learned a lot about the kinds of devices that she keeps track of in the inventory department.

   b. Katy learned about safety and about the symbols on electrical diagrams. She learned that electricity is extremely dangerous. The symbols tell what electrical devices will be in the final product.

   c. Electroserve uses a bar code to keep track of its products. An electronic machine reads the bar codes.

2. Salespeople keep the business coming in. Technicians can be promoted into the sales department once they know enough about the products.

REVIEW

1. Answers will vary.

CHAPTER 3

PREVIEW

1. Repairing Electrical Items

2. Electricity

   Electrical Repair

3. Electric Charge

   Current

   Static Electricity

   Energy and Power

4. Figure 3-1 Safety light.

Figure 3-2 Model of an atom.

Figure 3-3 Static electricity in hair.

Figure 3-4 Battery tester.

Figure 3-5 Switch inside hand-held tool.

Figure 3-6 Soldering an electronic connection.

Figure 3-7 Circuit diagram with symbols.

Figure 3-8 LED symbol.

Figure 3-9 Designing integrated circuits.

Figure 3-10 Using a CAD system to design.

QUESTION

1. How are electrical items repaired?

2. Answers will vary.

3. What is electricity?

4. Answers will vary.

5. What's involved in testing electrical items?

6. Answers will vary.

7. A battery tester. Answers will vary. It could be used to check batteries in a radio.

READ

1. Answers will vary. Terms should include *electricity*, *energy*, *electrons*, *atoms*, *protons*, and *neutrons*.

2. **Paragraph 1**

Topic Sentence: The quantity of electrons passing through a point is called the current.

Supporting Details: You can compare this current to water flowing through a pipe. Scientists use the letter *I* to stand for current.

Paragraph 2

Topic Sentence: Sometimes, the current has a short circuit.

Supporting Details: This problem occurs when the current in a machine runs around the parts that it is supposed to go through. A short circuit can damage equipment and must be repaired.

Paragraph 3

Topic Sentence: The current is measured in amperes, commonly called amps.

Supporting Details: Just one ampere is 6,250,000,000,000,000,000 electrons passing through a point in one second. Imagine how small an electron is!

Paragraph 4

Topic Sentence: Another important measure tells how much work an electric device can do.

Supporting Details: Voltage (V) tells how much potential energy a particular device has. A 1/2-volt battery can light a penlight but a big flashlight might need a 9-volt battery.

3. **Paragraph 1**

Topic Sentence: This kind of electricity is called static electricity.

Supporting Details: Figure 3-3 shows static electricity in action. The girl is standing next to a static generator. Her hair is standing on end. It seems to be trying to reach the generator. The generator has a negative charge. The hair has a positive charge. And the two opposites attract.

Paragraph 2

Topic Sentence: The example of the hair and the generator shows what a strong force an electric charge is.

Supporting Details: You are study electricity and electronics. You will learn about the movement of electrons. You will learn how to use electrical energy to do different kinds of work.

4. **Paragraph 1**

Topic Sentence: Electricity is one form of energy.

Supporting Details: Energy is the capacity to do work. Work comes from different forms of energy. When you pull a sled, you use mechanical energy. When you cook on a gas stove, you use heat energy. When you turn on a light, the bulb changes electrical energy into light energy.

Paragraph 2

Topic Sentence: Light bulbs usually have a measure that indicates how much power the bulb has.

Supporting Details: A bulb's power is measure in watts. A 40-watt bulb has less lighting power than a 100-watt bulb.

Paragraph 3

Topic Sentence: Another measure of power, horsepower, gives the units of power in an engine.

Supporting Detail: Each unit equals 745.7 watts.

5. Topic Sentence: The safety light operates on batteries.

Supporting Details: José tests the batteries first. To test the batteries, José uses a battery tester. The tester has two wires. The positive wire is connected to the end of the battery that has a plus sign. The negative wire is connected to the end that has a minus sign.

RECODE

1. Possible Answer: José has told you some of the basics and is showing you how to repair a safety light. A safety light is just like a flashlight, but it has one difference. It turns on automatically when the room darkens. José needs

to understand how the light works and to examine each part so that he can troubleshoot the problem.

2. Possible Answers:

    a. The safety-light repair was simple. Sometimes with other items, such as a toaster, the technician needs to refer to circuit diagrams to find possible trouble spots. The circuit diagrams are maps showing the inside of an item.

    b. Figure 3-7 contains symbols shown on a circuit diagram. Some of them have labels. Technicians learn how to read these symbols so that they can repair electrical items.

    c. The symbols are a diagram of how the current flows. The designer can show on the drawing where the electricity will flow freely and where it will be interrupted as with switches.

REVIEW

1. Answers will vary.

2. The defined boldface terms are as follows.

amp An abbreviation for *ampere*

ampere A unit of measure. An ampere is the measure of the intensity of current. Each ampere represents 6,250,000,000,000,000,000 electrons flowing through one point at one time.

atom The smallest unit of an element. The atom has a nucleus, or central part, surrounded by electrons. The nucleus contains protons.

charge To make something electrically negative or positive. Also, the property of something that allows it to have a negative or positive quality.

circuit A path through which electrical current flows.

circuit diagram A drawing that shows the circuit in a component or a device. The drawing shows symbols that indicate various characteristics of the circuit, for instance, how it will flow.

current A flow of electric charge.

electric charge See *charge*.

electricity A form of energy that comes from the movement of electrons and the interactions of electric charges.

electron A particle inside an atom, which has a negative electric charge. Electrons surround the nucleus, or central part, of the atom.

energy Power that can be used to do work. For example, electrical energy can toast bread in a toaster.

free electron An electron that is not trapped by the orbit of the nucleus in an atom. Free electrons can move between atoms. They form the basis of electricity.

horsepower A unit of power equal to 745.7 watts. Horsepower is usually used to describe the power of engines.

I The symbol for *current*.

negative Having an electric charge that is the same as that of an electron so that electrons are repelled. A minus sign (-) is used to indicate a negative charge.

neutron A unit inside the nucleus, or central part, of an atom. It is neutral and does not have either a negative or positive charge.

positive Having an electric charge that can attract electrons because the charge is the opposite of the negative charge within an electron. A plus sign (+) indicates a positive charge.

potential energy Energy that is available or stored in a place. Energy that is not from the movement of electrical current. A good example of potential energy is a spring that is tightly coiled. When let go, the stored energy releases the power of the spring.

proton A particle within an atom that has a positive electrical charge.

resistance The quality of a circuit that prevents electrons from flowing through it.

short circuit A path across a source. The path provides zero resistance to the electrical current so that the current goes around the devices in a circuit. A short circuit usually causes equipment failure.

solder To join two metal pieces together with a molten combination of tin and lead. Also, the material itself. When cool, the solder hardens and holds the connection fast.

static electricity Electricity accumulating in one place as opposed to electricity moving in a current.

V The abbreviation for *volt*.

voltage The amount of electric potential or volts.

watt A unit of electric power, as in a machine or a device such as a bulb.

REVIEW YOUR KNOWLEDGE

CHAPTER 1

1. A form of energy that comes from the movement of electrons and the interactions of electric charges.

2. The field of technology concerned with developing devices powered by the flow of electrons in active components, such as transistors.

3. Electronics

4. Computers and communications

5. c.

6. c.

7. F

8. T

CHAPTER 2

1. A list of items in stock.

2. A group of lines that can be read by a scanning device. The code usually represents one item and some information about it, such as price.

3. A diagram of how the electricity will flow in a device.

4. A series of steps for doing something.

5. Managers

6. d.

7. b.

8. T

9. F

CHAPTER 3

1. A negatively charged particle inside an atom.

2. The property of something that allows it to have a positive or negative quality when referring to electricity.

3. An electron that is not trapped by the orbit of the nucleus in an atom.

4. A path across a source that has zero resistance and allows the current to go around the devices in a circuit causing equipment failure.

5. Amperes

6. d.

7. c.

8. F

9. T

P A R T 4 *Answer Key*

SELF-CHECK 4-1

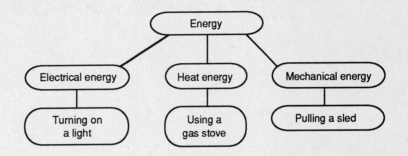

SELF-CHECK 4-2

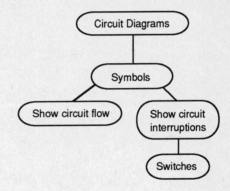

SELF-CHECK 4-3

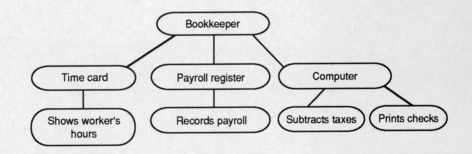

SELF-CHECK 4-4

    B. Electronics technician

        1. Manufacturing

        2. Sales and service

  II. (Next Main Idea)

SELF-CHECK 4-5

I. Electricity

    A. Electric charge

        1. Positive

        2. Negative

    B. Current

        1. Short circuit

        2. Measured in amperes

        3. Voltage measures potential energy

    C. Static electricity

    D. Energy and power

        1. Electrical energy

        2. Mechanical energy

        3. Heat energy

        4. Watts measure power in light bulbs

        5. Horsepower measures power in engines

II. (Next Main Idea)

PRACTICING PQ3R WITH CHAPTER 4

PREVIEW

1. Repairing Electronic Items

2. Electronics

    Repairing Electronic Machines

3. Computers

    Circuit Boards

    Understanding Computers

    Computer Hardware

    Computer Software

    How Small Is Small?

4. Figure 4-1 Computer console on dashboard.

    Figure 4-2 A computer monitor.

    Figure 4-3 A printed circuit board.

    Figure 4-4 Components on printed circuit board.

    Figure 4-5 A resistor.

    Figure 4-6 A diode.

Figure 4-7 Capacitors.

Figure 4-8 A microcircuit or microchip.

Figure 4-9 A software display.

QUESTION

1. How do you repair electronic items?

2. Answers will vary.

3. What is electronics?

4. Answers will vary.

5. How do you repair electronic machines?

6. Answers will vary.

7. A microcircuit or microchip. Possible Answer: television, cash registers, and computers.

READ

1. Answers will vary. Terms should include *electronic, computer, hardware, software, electronic circuits, central processing unit, monitor, keyboard, power supply, software,* and *programs.*

2. **Paragraph 1**

   Topic Sentence: Electricity is the field of technology that studies the movement of electrons.

   Supporting Details: Electronics is the field of technology that deals with electrons moving along conductors. Conductors are materials or substances that make an easy path for the flow of electricity.

   Paragraph 2

   Topic Sentence: Electronic devices also use many semiconductors.

   Supporting Details: Semiconductors are materials that fall somewhere between good conductors and good insulators. This means that they allow the flow of current but not as freely as conductors do.

3. **Paragraph 1**

   Topic Sentence: Computer hardware means all the parts of the computer that you can see and touch.

   Supporting Details: It also means all the electronic circuits inside the central processing unit of the computer.

   Paragraph 2

   Topic Sentence: Electroserve does not manufacture computers.

   Supporting Details: But the company does make products that use computers and other electronic parts. One of the most common parts, a printed circuit board, is made up of various materials that control the flow of electrons. Engineers design circuit boards to perform certain functions. Figure 4-3 shows a printed circuit board.

Paragraph 3

Topic Sentence: Circuit board technology is always advancing.

Supporting Details: The materials used to make boards have changed. The component parts are always being improved.

Paragraph 4

Topic Sentence: Electroserve uses microcircuits in its cash register products.

Supporting Details: Many of the circuits the company uses are integrated circuits (also called ICs). This means that on one board, a number of parts are integrated or connected to work together.

RECODE

1. Possible Answers:

   a. The difference between a typewriter and computer can be shown by typing one letter. The typewriter mechanically strikes the ribbon when you hit the letter. The computer gets the information in the form of bytes when the letter is pressed on the keyboard. The bytes of information are stored in the computer's memory and can be shown on the computer screen.

   b. The two main parts of a computer are its hardware and software.

2. Possible Answer:

   Lots of products became possible because of small circuit boards. Digital watches, calculators and other computer controls are now much more available for everyday use.

3.

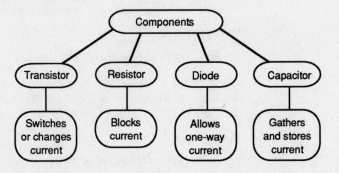

REVIEW

1. Answers will vary.

PRACTICING PQ3R WITH CHAPTER 5

PREVIEW

1. Working in Manufacturing

2. Filling Orders

   Planning

   Making the Product

   Sending out the Product

   Getting Paid

3. Using Machinery

   Quality Control

4. Figure 5-1 A cash register being used in a restaurant.

   Figure 5-2 A power ratchet with a charger.

   Figure 5-3 A maintenance contract.

   Figure 5-4 Minor purchases.

   Figure 5-5 An inventory card.

   Figure 5-6 An inventory report.

   Figure 5-7 A purchase order.

   Figure 5-8 An invoice.

   Figure 5-9 Checking supplies as they come in.

   Figure 5-10 Manufacturing machinery.

   Figure 5-11 Computer monitors being packed in Styrofoam before shipping.

   Figure 5-12 An order form and bill.

QUESTION

1. What is it like to work in manufacturing?

2. Answers will vary.

3. How do you fill orders?

4. Answers will vary.

5. What is involved in planning?

6. Answers will vary.

7. How do you make the product?

8. Answers will vary.

9. Cash register. Answers will vary.

READ

1. Answers will vary. Terms should include *manufacturing, assembling, housings, printed circuit boards, power supplies,* and *switches.*

2. **Paragraph 1**

   Topic Sentence: The manufacturing area fills orders for items.

Supporting Details: Sometimes, plant managers expect orders and start to manufacture for potential orders. This enables them to have inventory on hand to supply customers quickly.

Paragraph 2

Topic Sentence: When orders come in, plant managers look at the numbers.

Supporting Detail: If items are in stock, they will ship them. If they have manufactured the item before, they will tell manufacturing to make the necessary number.

Paragraph 3

Topic Sentence: If, however, the item requires a new design or just a change in design, they send the job to design.

Supporting Details: The designers plan the item. They also get the customer's approval of the final design if necessary. Then design sends the plans to manufacturing's planning department.

3. **Paragraph 1**

Topic Sentence: The first stage of manufacturing is planning.

Supporting Detail: Planning includes taking designs and instructions and figuring out how the project will go.

Paragraph 2

Topic Sentence: The planning department sees if it can make all parts of the item in-house.

Supporting Detail: Often, Electroserve needs to buy parts, make some of the parts, and assemble the item.

Paragraph 3

Topic Sentence: Manufacturing keeps its own inventory system.

Supporting Detail: It also does its own purchasing, receiving, and storing of supplies.

4. Topic Sentence: Two basic types of inventory purchases are made by the manufacturing department.

Supporting Details: When Benjamin buys an item that costs less than $100, he is making a minor purchase. When he buys an item that costs more than $100, he is making a major purchase.

RECODE

1. Possible Answers:

   a. Benjamin has to keep careful track of what he needs. If he orders too much, he will use up valuable cash and storage space. He has to know how much stock he has on hand.

   b. It is just as bad to run out of an item. That wastes valuable worker time and may make a customer's order late.

   c. If you know how fast an item is used and how long delivery of an item takes, you will know when to order.

2.

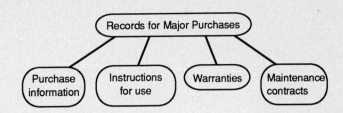

REVIEW

1. Answers will vary.

2. The defined boldface term is as follows:

   housing The outside shell of a machine or device that serves as a cover. The housing also holds the interior parts in place either because the housing has slots and openings or because parts are attached to it.

PRACTICING PQ3R WITH CHAPTER 6

PREVIEW

1. Assembling Electronic Products

2. Getting the Parts Together

   Finishing the Product

3. Job Numbers

   Assembling the Parts

   Basic Wiring

   Electrical Wire

   Connecting Wire

   Electronic Wire

   Inserting Printed Circuit Boards

4. Figure 6-1 A supply area in a large manufacturing company.

   Figure 6-2 A technician assembling computer monitors.

   Figure 6-3 Assembly technicians at work in a large manufacturing company.

   Figure 6-4 Housing for a television.

   Figure 6-5 A wire from an electric drill.

   Figure 6-6 Printed wire on a circuit board.

   Figure 6-7 Stranded wire at a construction site.

   Figure 6-8 Cable showing stranded wire held together.

   Figure 6-9 A technician working on power lines.

Figure 6-10 An electrician taping wires together for a ceiling fixture.

Figure 6-11 The UL symbol.

Figure 6-12 Precision soldering of electronic parts.

Figure 6-13 A fiberglass printed circuit board.

Figure 6-14 Switches on components on a printed circuit board.

QUESTION

1. a. Answers will vary.

   b. Answers will vary.

READ

1. (a) kits, (b) assemble, (c) housing, (d) boards

2. Possible Answer: The supply room of the assembly area has all the parts needed to assemble a product.

3. **Paragraph 1**

   Topic Sentence: Solid wire does not bend easily.

   Paragraph 2

   Topic Sentence: Wire that must be flexed is made of strands.

4. a. F

   b. T

   c. F

5. **Paragraph 1**

   Possible Answer: Since solid wire does not bend easily, it is used where the wire will stay in place and not be moved often.

   Paragraph 2

   Possible Answer: Wire that must be bent easily is made up of strands held together.

   Paragraph 3

   Possible Answer: Cable is made up of groups of stranded wire held together.

6. (a) bend, (b) strands, (c) covering, (d) cable, (e) insulated, (f) resistance.

7. **Paragraph 1**

   Possible Answer: In a typical factory assembly line, there is a belt along which a product moves while workers attach parts at various points on the line.

   Paragraph 2

   Possible Answer: Electroserve's assembly department has workers who assemble a whole product by themselves.

   Paragraph 3

   Possible Answer: As in an assembly line, the workers line up the products but they put them together themselves.

8. (a) plugs, (b) electrons, (c) circuit board, (d) copper, (e) silver

9. a. F

   b. T

   c. T

RECODE

1.

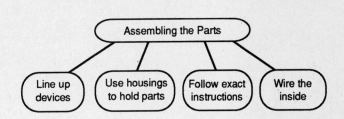

2.

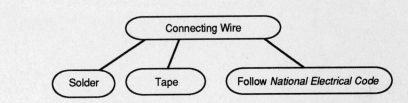

REVIEW

1. The defined boldface words are as follows.

   cable A group of wires twisted together.

   component A part of the whole. Two examples of electronic components are a transistor or a diode.

   conduct To allow electricity to flow through.

   conductor A substance or material that provides an easy path for a flow of energy, such as electricity.

   housing The outside shell of a machine or device that serves as a cover. The housing also holds the interior parts in place either because the housing has slots and openings or because parts are attached to it.

   insulator A material that will not conduct electricity. Rubber and plastics are good insulators.

   kit A setup of parts that when assembled complete a machine or a part of a machine.

   resistance The quality of a circuit that prevents electrons from flowing through it.

   solder To join two metal pieces together with a molten combination of tin and lead. Also, the material itself. When cool, the solder hardens and holds the connection fast.

   strand One piece of wire meant to be twisted or put together with other wire to form flexible wire.

superconductor Any of various materials that have virtually zero resistance. Superconductors are playing an important role in the development of new electronic products.

REVIEW YOUR KNOWLEDGE

CHAPTER 4

1. Conductor

2. An extremely small piece of material, such as silicon, upon which a microcircuit is placed.

3. 8

4. An electronic circuit package that puts a number of electronic devices together. Examples of such devices are resistors, transistors, diodes, and capacitors.

5. Resistors, transistors, diodes, and capacitors.

6. d.

7. a.

8. T

9. F

CHAPTER 5

1. A shell that covers the central processing unit, cards, and power supply of a computer.

2. Planning

3. A certificate that guarantees that the manufacturer will be responsible for a part or machine for a specified period of time under normal use.

4. An agreement that says that a repair person or manufacturer will service and repair equipment for a specified period of time.

5. c.

6. d.

7. T

8. F

CHAPTER 6

1. A setup that has all the parts to assemble something.

2. A single piece of wire that does not bend easily.

3. Flexible wire made up of several pieces of wire held together by a covering.

4. A conductor allows current to flow through or along it, while a resistor blocks the flow of current.

5. d.

6. F

7. T

8. F

9. T

10. F

Answer Key

SELF-CHECK 5-1

1. Main Idea: José learned about electricity.

   Supporting Details: Electricity is energy. It is energy that comes from the movement of tiny particles called electrons. Everything—from air to wood is made of atoms. Even people are made up of atoms. Electrons move inside atoms. Also inside atoms are protons and neutrons.

2. Pictures will vary.

SELF-CHECK 5-2

Major Purchases

Record of Purchase	Major Functions
Purchase information	To keep records of all items bought and prices
Instructions on use	For training and repairing
Warranties	For manufacturer's guarantee in case of problems
Maintenance contracts	In case of equipment breakdowns

SELF-CHECK 5-3

Electronic Components

Component	Purpose
Resistor	Blocks current flow
Transistor	Increases, changes, or switches flow
Diode	Allows flow in only one direction
Capacitor	Collects and stores electric charges

SELF-CHECK 5-4

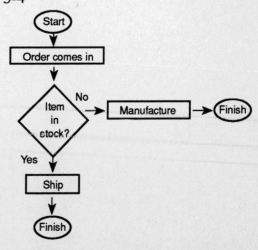

SELF-CHECK 5-5

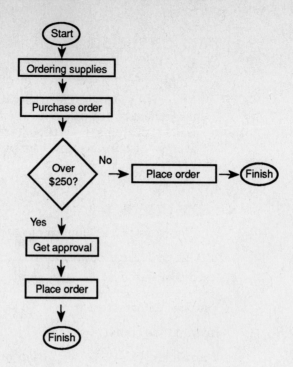

SELF-CHECK 5-6

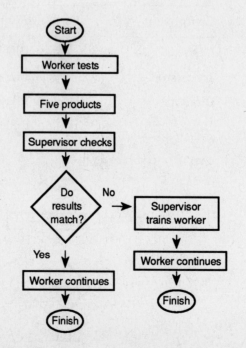

PREVIEW

1. Testing Electrical and Electronic Products

2. Testing Procedures

   Function Testing

   Final Check

3. Figure 7-1 A testing department.

   Figure 7-2 A testing checklist.

   Figure 7-3 Electric meters on a two-family house.

   Figure 7-4 An analog watch (left) and a digital watch (right).

   Figure 7-5 An ammeter.

   Figure 7-6 Five common battery sizes.

   Figure 7-7 A voltmeter.

   Figure 7-8 An ohmmeter.

   Figure 7-9 Analog (left) and digital (right) multimeters.

   Figure 7-10 An oscilloscope.

   Figure 7-11 A reading on a battery tester.

   Figure 7-12 A function checklist.

   Figure 7-13 A computer testing station at a state-run automotive emissions testing center.

   Figure 7-14 A computerized testing center at a manufacturer.

QUESTION

1. a. Answers will vary.

   b. Answers will vary.

   c. Answers will vary.

READ

1. **Paragraph 1**

   Possible Answer: The testing department has a procedure for checking each product.

   Paragraph 2

   Possible Answer: The technician uses a checklist to make sure each product gets all needed tests.

Paragraph 3

Possible Answer: Since the technician and supervisor have to sign the checklist, everyone tends to be responsible.

2. **Paragraph 1**

Topic Sentence: A meter measures something.

Supporting Details: Parking meters measure time. Electrical meters on a house measure the amount of electricity used by the residents. Figure 7-3 shows electrical meters on a two-family house. Each part of the house has a separate meter so that each family pays for its own electricity.

Paragraph 2

Topic Sentence: Meters show numbers on a dial.

Supporting Details: The display can be either analog or digital. An analog display shows the numbers with marks between them to indicate a certain amount. A digital display shows only one amount, or measure. A good way to understand the difference between the two displays is to compare two common types of watches. An analog watch has a circular dial with marks or numbers all around. Hands point to the current time on the dial. A digital watch displays the time in one set of numbers or digits. Figure 7-4 shows both types of watches.

3. (a)amperes, (b)amps, (c) current, (d) direct current, (e) alternating current

RECODE

1. Possible Answer: A voltmeter measures the force that causes electrons to flow. It has two wires that are color-coded: black stands for negative and red for positive. A voltmeter can be connected to a device such as a battery. The higher the volts, the more power a device such as a battery can handle.

2. **Paragraph 1**

Possible Answer: Both the technician and the supervisor are responsible for making sure all items are checked off on the checklist.

Paragraph 2

Possible Answer: The serial number for each electronic product means that testing problems can be traced back to each technician and supervisor.

Paragraph 3

Possible Answer: Technicians use testers to check the current and resistance in electrical and electronic devices.

3.

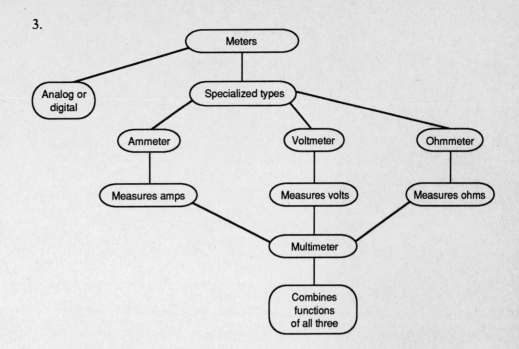

4.

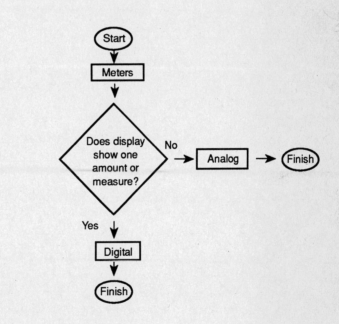

5. I. Testing Procedures

   A. Testing system

   B. Testing responsibility

   C. Meters used as testers

      l. Ammeter

      2. Voltmeter

3. Ohmmeter

4. Multimeter

D. Other testers

1. Oscilloscope

2. Battery tester

E. Function testing

F. Final check

II. Next Main Idea

REVIEW

1. The defined boldface words are as follows.

AC The abbreviation for *alternating current*.

alternating current A type of current flow in which the electrons first move in one direction and then move in the reverse direction.

ammeter A meter that measures current in amps.

amp An abbreviation for *ampere*.

ampere A unit of measure. An ampere is the measure of the intensity of current. Each ampere represents 6,250,000,000,000,000,000 electrons flowing through one point at one time.

analog Represented by measurable quantities. An analog watch has numbers or marks equally spaced to represent the passage of time.

DC The abbreviation for *direct current*.

digit A single numerical symbol. In computers, digits are usually either zero or one.

digital Representing information as a series of digits. A digital watch shows the time in a series of numbers, rather than by the position of hands on a dial.

direct current A type of electric current in which the electrons flow in one direction only.

multimeter A measuring or testing device that serves all the functions of an ammeter, ohmmeter, and a voltmeter.

ohm A unit of measurement that equals one unit of the resistance of a conductor to the flow of electrical current.

ohmmeter A measuring and testing device that measures ohms.

oscilloscope An electronic instrument that displays the wave action of a current on a screen. Oscilloscopes have a cathode-ray tube for the display.

tester A device or machine that measures or tests something, such as the qualities of a circuit.

testing device See *tester*.

volt A unit of measure equal to the electric potential. It is measured between the ends of a conductor with the resistance of one ohm and with a current of one ampere flowing through it.

voltage The amount of electric potential or volts.

voltmeter A testing device that measures voltage.

PRACTICING PQ3R WITH CHAPTER 8

PREVIEW

1. Dealing With Customers

   Handling Work Safely

   Testing Products On-Site

   Doing Proper Paperwork

2. 8

3. Figure 8-1 A technician using an electronic address book to call for an appointment.

   Figure 8-2 A well-lighted menu board.

   Figure 8-3 An electrician working on a circuit breaker box.

   Figure 8-4 An electrician working on wires after the power supply has been turned off.

   Figure 8-5 An on-site function checklist.

   Figure 8-6 A work order form.

   Figure 8-7 A daily schedule for a technician.

   Figure 8-8 A bill for service time.

QUESTION

1. a. Answers will vary.

   b. Answers will vary.

   c. Answers will vary.

   d. Answers will vary.

READ

1. **Paragraph 1**

   Topic Sentence: The electrician will actually install the menu board to its power supply.

   Paragraph 2

   Topic Sentence: Before installing the actual board, the electrician works on the power supply.

2. (a) customers, (b) appointment, (c) business, (d) clean

RECODE

1.

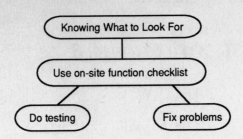

2. Possible Answer: A problem shows up at the site when the switches are hooked up incorrectly. Joyce can solve the problem by relabeling the switches. She does this and the board works fine.

3. I. On-Site Service

    A. Dealing with customers

        1. Show good manners

        2. Follow five rules

    B. Handling work safely

        1. Know the rules of safety

            a. Follow codes

            b. Turn power off

        2. Use tools with rubber handles

    C. Testing products on-site

        1. Use function checklist

        2. Fix any problems

    D. Doing proper paperwork

        1. Fill out work order form

        2. Get manager's signature

  II. (Next Main Idea)

REVIEW

1. Answers will vary but should include most of the five rules given on page 95 of the *Knowledge Base* and performing an on-site function check.

PRACTICING PQ3R WITH CHAPTER 9

PREVIEW

1. Safety in Electricity and Electronics

2. Understanding Electricity

   Handling Electricity

3. Figure 9-1 A display of lightning.

   Figure 9-2 Lightning hitting the ground on a prairie.

   Figure 9-3 Power lines downed after a tornado.

   Figure 9-4 Tools with insulated handles.

   Figure 9-5 Wires hooked to a testing meter.

   Figure 9-6 A technician wearing safe clothing.

   Figure 9-7 A grounded outlet.

QUESTION

1. a. Answers will vary.

   b. Answers will vary.

READ

1. Possible Answer: Electricity has a lot of power. It comes from the movement of electrons. Lightning bolts are displays of electricity that can kill very quickly. A strong electric shock can also kill or injure someone.

2. (a) power, (b) conductors, (c) conduct, (d) grounded

3. Topic Sentence: Not all electrical charges pose a danger.

   Supporting Details: Sometimes, particularly in cold weather, you may get a small shock from touching a fabric. This static electricity does not injure you. It just reminds you that electricity is all around us.

RECODE

1. Possible Answer: Since electricity can harm you, it is important to understand it so that you can avoid getting shocks.

2.

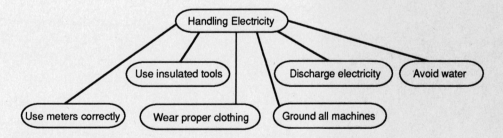

3.
   I. Safety in Electricity and Electronics

   A. Understanding electricity

   1. The power of electricity

      a. Lightning

      b. Electric shocks

   2. Static electricity

B. Handling electricity

    1. Proper use of tools

    2. Proper clothing

    3. Avoiding water

II. (Next Main Idea)

4.

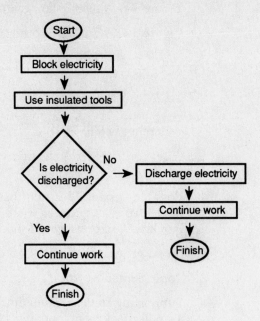

REVIEW

1. The defined boldface words are as follows.

arc To cross over a gap, as in a streak of electricity. As a safety measure, any equipment likely to arc should be disconnected and discharged.

discharge To remove the stored electric charge from, as in a battery.

electrocute To kill by electricity.

ground An electrical conductor attached to the earth. Also, to connect electricity to such a conductor. A grounded outlet is considered safe.

shock The startling feeling caused by electric current going through the body or any one it parts.

static electricity Electricity accumulating in one place as opposed to electricity moving in a current.

2. Answers will vary.

REVIEW YOUR KNOWLEDGE

CHAPTER 7

1. A device or machine that measures or tests something, such as the qualities of a circuit.

2. Analog displays have measurable quantities as on a watch with hour, minute, and second hands. Digital displays have just one series of digits.

3. ammeter, voltmeter, and ohmmeter

4. A unit of measure of the intensity of current.

5. F

6. T

7. T

8. F

CHAPTER 8

1. Be polite; schedule appointments; don't interfere with business; respect others' opinions; clean up after yourself.

2. A box through which electricity is distributed after passing through switches.

3. For safety. The codes avoid the misuse of electricity.

4. As insulation against the flow of electricity.

5. Because the company is likely to bill the technician's hours to the customer.

6. F

7. T

8. T

CHAPTER 9

1. A form of energy that comes from the movement of electrons and the interactions of electric charges.

2. Electricity

3. It crosses over a gap and can cause injury.

4. To avoid getting shocked by stored electric charges.

5. F

6. T

7. T